CW00938130

Dawn Chorus

DAWN CHORUS

Joan Wyndham

Joan Wyndham —

Virago

A *Virago* Book

First published in Great Britain by
Virago Press 2004

A CIP catalogue record for this book
is available from the British Library

ISBN 1 84408 152 4

Typeset in Bembo by M Rules
Printed and bound in Great Britain
by Clays Ltd, St Ives plc

Virago Press
An imprint of
Time Warner Book Group UK
Brettenham House
Lancaster Place
London WC2E 7EN

www.virago.co.uk

THE FIRST THREE YEARS of my childhood were spent in a vast Victorian country house in Wiltshire called Clouds. Built entirely of green sandstone, it boasted forty bedrooms, and a kitchen so far from the dining room that a miniature railway track had to be built to carry food from one place to the other. Luckily, tepid meals were the norm in those days.

It had been built by my great-grandfather, Percy Wyndham, who had been thrown out of the ancestral home, Petworth, as soon as his jealous elder brother inherited it. His aim had been to make a new home for the Wyndhams whose ambience would be warm and hospitable, the exact opposite of the family seat, where he had spent a miserable childhood.

His mother, Mary, a religious fanatic, had allowed her children no contact with the outside world. She had

1

strange ideas of what was sinful – reading novels was for-bidden, and if occasionally they managed to escape to London and went to a ball, they were not allowed to dance the waltz. In fact, visits to the capital were rare. There is one rather astonishing story concerning Mary's phobias. Having once cut her finger in a London cab, she vowed never to use one again – so, on her rare visits to London, she was obliged to commandeer a whole train to carry herself, her carriage and horses, and a retinue of servants.

Percy spent many years searching for the perfect setting for his new family seat and finally found it in Wiltshire. It was already occupied by a small house named Clowde, but this he demolished and work began on a new building; the name was changed to Clouds. He employed one of the leading architects of the day, Philip Webb, and together they worked on it for nearly ten years. It was built of sandstone from a local quarry at a cost of eighty thousand pounds. This was a huge amount of money for those days, but the house was enormous, a made-to-order ancestral home, magnificent but not pretentious. It faced south-west with an unbroken view of green parkland and meadow while the other three sides were shadowed by trees. The inside of the house was decorated almost entirely in blue and white, the only other colours coming from the magnificent William Morris carpets and hangings. In the centre of the house there was a great hall with a grand staircase leading up from it. Outside, Percy had done everything possible to make it seem manorial, with peacocks on the lawn, hunters in the stables and tenants in the adjoining cottages.

According to family legend, during the final stages of building, there was a rather worrying incident. The family were all away and the workers were putting the finishing touches to the great hall when a woman dressed entirely in black knocked at the west door and Neil, the builder, let her in. She looked around as if sniffing the air and said, 'This house will be no more in less than four years' time.' But this was soon forgotten, and Percy and Madeleine, his wife, finally moved into their new home, full of hope and excitement. This couple were unique in one way. Unlike most rich aristocrats at that time, they were passionately interested in everything to do with the arts. They were also famous for their house parties and lavish hospitality – artists and politicians, friends and family were welcomed with open arms, and the guests ranged from Arthur Balfour, the prime minister, to Oscar Wilde and Bosie, whose thank-you letters were always written in medieval English. With such illustrious guests, Clouds soon became known as the 'House of the Age'.

By the time I was born in 1921, much of this glory had departed and my memories of it are hazy. Most of my time was spent in the upstairs nursery with a fierce nanny for company and a wooden rocking-horse. I, of course, only came up to its stirrups, but one day I hoped I would be big enough to ride it properly. I had noticed a hole in the saddle where you could stick a wooden pommel, so I knew I wouldn't fall off. I also remember endlessly skating around the lino floor on my tin potty under the stern gaze of Nanny, who was waiting hopefully for the arrival of what she called 'number twos'. Of all the grand rooms downstairs, I remember only one: the huge library. I'm lying curled up on the floor on a sheepskin rug and my mother is bending over me. In one hand she holds a large book and in the other a pencil, which she pushes down its spine; I chortle gleefully as I watch it pop out the other end.

However, I had no need of memories when it came to creating a clearer picture of Clouds and its owners. Down the generations, no one had thrown away a single scrap of paper. I found, much to my delight, trunks full of letters and diaries, boxes of Marconigrams (telegrams), visitors' books, memos and lists.

I also found a fascinating copy of the Wyndham family tree, going back to our first ancestor, Ailwardus de Wymondham in 1066. Wymondham is a small town in Norfolk, so I guess it had been grabbed by Ailwardus as part of his perks for supporting the Norman Conquest. A few generations later, the name was changed to Wyndham. My ancestors seem to have had chequered careers in politics ranging from Treasurer of England and Chancellor of the Exchequer in 1266, to 'Master of the Buckhounds', to 'Secretary of War and Knight for the King's Body' in 1700. Some were less fortunate – John Wyndham, for example, a strong supporter of Henry VI, was knighted at the battle of Stoke in 1487, but beheaded in 1502.

All marriages, of course, were correctly recorded until you come to the Clouds period when something rather unusual happened: lovers and intimates began to be included alongside legitimate husbands and wives.

So we get 'Hugo, (Lord Elcho), lover of Hermione, Duchess of Leinster,' and 'Lady Angela Forbes, and Mary Wyndham, intimate of J. Balfour (child by Wilfred Scawen Blunt)'. Even the virtuous Madeleine features as 'Beloved of Harry Cust, and lover of Wilfred Scawen Blunt' even though the latter, known as 'Society's pet tom-cat' had already given her daughter an illegitimate child. And this in the Victorian age, when even piano legs were considered immodest without concealing-wraps.

Percy, it seemed, was an old-fashioned dandy, usually dressed in a nankeen tailcoat and spats. He kept his eau-de-Cologne in a special little niche just outside the dining room and never offered an arm to his dinner partner without first having a couple of quick dabs. He also had a filthy temper and was known to have once shot his gamekeeper in the foot for picking up the wrong pheasant. By contrast, his wife Madeleine was almost saintly: a warm, eccentric lady, admired and loved by all. She liked to dabble in the visual arts; watercolours, etchings and even enamelling – working at what the family called her 'scrattle' table. She would sit there for hours on end, scrattling away with a flock of tame doves circling her head, much to the dismay of the servants who had to clean their mess off the William Morris carpets. But her worst habit was to write long and probably rather irritating letters to any friend or relative who was doing up their house – for instance:

> *Dearest Mary,*
> *I send you a bit of cheap cream damask as a table cover to replace the yellow silk you put on the <u>wrong side out</u>! Also a bit of blue – a remnant – for <u>anywhere</u> – maybe over those red chairs that swear so terribly with all the <u>greens</u>! But perhaps this will not match the lovely green silk piano cover??? <u>I fear it will not!!</u> But then you <u>could</u> use it for the table cover?? In case <u>the cream damask does not come on time</u>!*

But she also found time to create a home from home for a small coterie of friends known as the Souls, an exclusive little group dedicated to intellectual pursuits and their own egos. Apart from the Wyndhams, certain other families were at the core of this clique – the Tennants, Adeanes, Elchos, Windsors and Grenfells. Among the female Souls, Margot Tennant, Diana Duff-Cooper and Cynthia Asquith were famed for their beauty, wit and intelligence, while the two most famous members were frequent visitors – Prime Minister Arthur Balfour and Viceroy to India George Curzon.

Hunting and fishing were taboo for the Souls, as were baccarat and chemin-de-fer. Gambling and racing were regarded as vulgar and extravagant but golf, tennis and bicycling were popular. An ascetic approach to life was a requirement, and most of the group adopted frugality. Travelling by train was often by third class, food was simple, and most were teetotallers. This was a time when upper-class ladies often spent over ten thousand pounds a year on their wardrobe but Souls women scorned what they called the 'swansdown and sables' of Society and chose to dress simply. They were all avid readers, everything from Dickens to Henry James, and patronised avant-garde artists such as Burne-Jones, Sargent, Watts and Whistler.

It was inevitable that less enlightened members of the aristocracy, such as the super-smart 'Marlborough House Set', regarded them as a self-indulgent bunch worthy of mockery. The presence of a clever woman even in their own ranks seemed to make them nervous: a prospective suitor of the beautiful young Soul, Mary Wyndham, was heard to say, 'A very nice filly, but she's read too many books for me!' On the other hand, they had many admirers among the more intelligent members of Society: 'Thanks to the Souls,' said Lady Violet Bonham Carter, 'it was no longer fashionable to be dull.'

There was certainly nothing dull about the Clouds house parties where the Souls were frequent guests. These began at Easter and continued throughout the legendary long summers of late Victorian times. One grateful guest who had enjoyed a 'Saturday-to-Monday' (the word 'weekend' was never used) describes the 'spacious, lounging, talking-all-day life, with grand dinner parties to follow'. It was the custom in those days for women to withdraw when dinner ended, leaving the men to linger for hours over port and cigars. But the Souls would have none of that. Sexual segregation was taboo: they believed that men and women should be able to associate freely without the necessity of falling in love or the fear of social scandal. As a result, platonic friendships became the order of the day, and after-dinner bed-hopping was replaced with pillow-fights, apple-pie beds or battles with wet sponges.

But on a more serious level their main passion was for after-dinner games, such as Charades, Telegrams and something called Clubs (an advanced form of Twenty Questions). Best of all, they enjoyed word games that gave them a chance to show off; Lexicon, played in French or German, was a favourite. In fact, most of their games needed the participants to have some knowledge of literature, history or languages, so outsiders tended to steer clear of them. They even had a special language of their own – 'Gangspeak' – with lots of bitchery and private jokes. A rather uncomfortable heart-to-heart talk was known as 'Having a Dentist'. A howler so dreadful, it could never sink to oblivion was a 'Floater', while a gorgeous, carefree time was a 'Swim-gloat'. Although many hours seemed to be passed in the pursuit of fun and freedom, this was underpinned nevertheless by a very stern philosophy of life founded on Christianity, patriotism, and the virtues of courage and optimism.

Naturally enough, with life so full of the demands of hospitality, no one at Clouds gave a second thought to the strange lady in black and her frightening prediction.

The winter of 1888 was one of the coldest in living memory and on 6 January, early in the morning, a sleepy servant put a scuttle full of ashes into a housemaid's cupboard. Unfortunately, some of them were still glowing and there was paper in the scuttle too. By seven o'clock the whole house was ablaze. The huge central hall made a perfect funnel, with flames roaring up from the ground floor to the roof. The nearest horsedrawn fire engine was twenty miles away at Salisbury. There were no telephones and the telegraph services were not operating at such an early hour so grooms galloped out from the stables, but it took them hours to reach the fire brigade. The roads that morning were like glass and the horses that drew the engine fell three times and were too badly hurt to carry on. They were replaced by fresh teams from nearby farms who went galloping on, slipping and sliding on the icy roads and seeing ahead of them, the enormous pillar of fire that Clouds had become. By the time they arrived, it was already too late: fire had engulfed the whole house.

By great good fortune, the family and its retinue had all escaped. Grandchildren in the top-floor nurseries were swaddled in wet blankets with sponges in their mouths and carried downstairs by their nannies whose shoes were almost burnt through on the red-hot stairs. Meanwhile, servants and villagers rushed in and out of the burning building, dragging out anything they thought valuable. They considered the billiard table to be the rarest object in the house so it was the first thing to be hauled on to the lawn. Valuable pictures and William Morris carpets followed, but the beautiful Burne-Jones paintings of angels that lined the staircase were all destroyed. Meanwhile Madeleine wandered distractedly round the garden, wringing her hands and crying, 'Oh, my Bible! Oh, my canaries!'

Although the inside of the house was totally destroyed, many of the outside walls, being three feet thick and fashioned from sandstone, remained intact. As a result, the indomitable Percy decided to rebuild it so that it was identical to the old house in every detail. Meanwhile, the family moved into the servants' quarters, designed by Webb the architect as a separate building. Although they didn't contain a bathroom, the family found them surprisingly comfortable. This they put down to Webb's socialist inclinations, which they considered deplorable – but were thankful for the results.

Two years later, the phoenix rose from the ashes. The Wyndhams moved back in and a huge party was thrown to celebrate, with the usual mix of artists, writers, politicians and family, plus a few of the surviving Souls. Isadora Duncan danced in the great hall. Life resumed its former happy, ordered pattern but one more tragedy lay in wait for Madeleine. Only six months after they had celebrated their golden wedding anniversary, Percy became seriously ill and died. Madeleine elected to stay on, but Clouds now belonged to their eldest son, George, who was known to the press at the age of forty-seven as 'the handsomest man in England'.

His brief political life had ended in failure. He had been made chief secretary to Ireland and was full of romantic visions for that country's future, particularly because Edward Fitzgerald, the famous revolutionary leader, had been his great-grandfather. But George lacked the capacity to carry these visions forward, and made a number of miscalculations concerning Home Rule policy that prompted Balfour to ask for his resignation in 1905.

Fed up with politics, George was only too happy to take on the duties of a landowner, running a huge house, farming two and a half thousand acres and looking after the well-being of his staff and tenants. He also made several alterations to Clouds, turning the unwanted nurseries into a library and building a chapel for his ultra-religious wife Sybil in part of the servants' quarters. This was done partly out of respect for her religion but also to thank her for the wonderfully civilised way she had accepted his mistress, Gay Windsor, who had once been her good friend. Not only did she continue to give George her love and support, she remained friendly with Gay.

Years passed with this arrangement in place until one day George decided to take his mistress on a little trip to Paris where they stayed at the Hôtel Lotti. Perhaps he was getting a little bit bored with her or maybe she had pleaded a headache – whatever the reason, one night he left her sleeping and went off in search of a brothel. Impressed by this handsome milord *anglais*, Madame no doubt allowed him the pick of the bunch, not realising how unused he was to professional titillation. His first orgasm brought on a heart-attack and he died soon after in the prostitute's bed. By the time his friends found him, rigor mortis had set in. They carried him back, stiff as a board, and had considerable difficulty in manoeuvring him through the glass doors of the Hôtel Lotti.

His mother seemed unable to give this event its appropriate significance. In her diaries almost every other page is a loving obituary to some dead pet – dogs, horses or birds. 'Darling little Sooty died today – buried under the yew tree. Alas! Alas! Alas!' For George there were only six words: 'George died in Paris. Was buried.' A canary would have rated more – but for George, who had broken the rules, there could be no 'Alas! Alas! Alas!'.

My father, Dick, was ten when his uncle George died. A typical tomboy, fond of dogs and horses, he was known as Dirty Dick and his brother Grubby George. Judging by his letters from school, spelling was not one of his strong points. In a letter to Madeleine, dated 'August. I do not no', he writes, 'Dear Gam-Gam, Orfly pleased with the preysents, speshly the droring book.'

Next came Wellington – a school some considered to be even better than Eton. Dick enjoyed his time there immensely and even learnt to spell.

Dearest Mud and Dad, he writes.
We play rugger this term and it is simply lovely. The best part is when we have a loose scrum and we all push and kick and shove and fight. This morning we had fire practice, which is ripping fun. We fairly fly down the fire shute, just like the one we have at Clouds. In the evenings, we play Pounce or go to the cinematograph Casino. I do wish you and

Gam-Gam could come and see me once, it would be ripping
fun. I could show you all around the school and show you
my garden and the balloon factory. By the way, Mud, can
you send me your best recipe for Bread Sauce. Now I must
stop for there is no more to say. Lots of love from Dickie

Unfortunately he only lasted a year at Wellington. There
was a puzzling letter from his headmaster, which said, 'Dick is
a good boy really, so perhaps one day he will grow out of this.'
Another letter contains a possible clue to the meaning of 'this'.

Darling Pa and Mud,
There is an orfly nice master called Padstow. When I go
out into the town, he often follows me and walks beside
me. He spits every ten minutes and makes unconcealed
funny little ittywit noises. (Ittywit was the name of
Dick's puppy) *He told me he is very poor and lives in*
one tiny room with only an artificial fire, and he would
really like it if I would come and visit him there. He says
he has lots of interesting things to show me! Please ask
Gam-Gam for a really good recipe for Bread and Butter
Pudding. Love, Dickie

After leaving Wellington Dick, like others of his class, had
three possible choices: politics, the army or the Church.

Politics would have been a cushy choice as the House sat for six months only, from the end of the foxhunting season to just before the start of grouse-shooting, but Dick felt that the army would be more glamorous and exciting. (He didn't even consider the Church.) He went to Sandhurst and soon became known as the academy's untidiest cadet. His uniform was ill-fitting, his buttons permanently undone, the art of puttee-winding was beyond him, and on one famous occasion he turned up on parade wearing his bedroom slippers. In spite of all this – or maybe because of it – he was very popular with his fellow cadets: when his favourite dog died, they gave it a military funeral.

Soon after leaving Sandhurst, he became a captain in the King's Royal Rifle Corps. When war broke out in 1914, his regiment was sent to the Front. Meanwhile, Madeleine stayed on at Clouds with Dick's parents, Guy and Minnie. Apart from Dick and his brother, Grubby George, she had four other grandsons with curious nick-names, given them by their adoring parents, Bim, Yvo, Ego and Perfoo, all of whom were killed in their twenties during the first two years of the war. Only Dick survived the trenches. Amazingly, Madeleine refused to admit the horror of it all. She wrote in her diary, 'Darling Perfoo! Gay, debonair, Fortune's darling, is dead! He was shot through the head, leading his men out of a wood. How glorious his death is!' Even stranger was a letter written to her daughter Mary, who was heartbroken by the deaths of both her sons: 'My dearest Mary, you have the <u>joy</u> that is beyond all joys. The knowledge that you have safely <u>lodged and landed</u> in <u>Heaven</u> two of the most beautiful darling and loving sons who were ever born into this world.' Joy? What joy could there be for a woman half crazy with grief?

My father Dick, thank God, had no such delusions. 'There were times,' he wrote to his parents, 'when I found war frightfully exciting but at others, it was just horrible slow murder.' In May 1915, his regiment was sent to defend the Ypres salient:

Moving to new positions, we naturally supposed that the RE had prepared perfect trenches with a high bullet-proof parapet, plenty of dugouts and good barbed wire entanglements. Instead we found a parapet that didn't even cover our shoulders, no dugouts, and no barbed wire. Five a.m. the shelling started and the Boche had our exact range. All next day they rained shells on us. People were buried alive in the trenches and horrible wounds inflicted. There were also small guns only four or five hundred yards away from us firing point blank. The men called these whizz-bangs. Five days in the firing line without a rest, we were pretty well done up. The Canadians were wonderfully brave, staying in their trenches until they were nearly all buried or hit. Then the

Germans came on and bayoneted them as they tried to
dig themselves out.

One of my company's jobs was to carry boxes of
ammunition to the firing line, marching dead slow for two
miles under shellfire. It was pretty warm, I can tell you.
One thing that amazed me was the amount of
unaccountable blunders made by our Commanding
Officers. It was quite amusing, like a Sandhurst Field Day
gone wrong. Just as we were settling down to our dinner,
there would come the well-known cry. '"A" Company!
Ready to move off at a moment's notice!' Five minutes
later it would be cancelled. When we finally set off for our
new trenches, it was already twelve p.m., and owing to our
guide being rather foolish, we didn't arrive till two thirty
a.m. The order came to dig ourselves in. We thought this
seemed rather funny since dawn broke at three a.m. We
supposed our trenches must be well out of view of the
enemy but no sooner had we started to dig than the
adjutant came running up in a fearful state. 'Tell the men
to stop work at once,' he screamed. 'For God's sake –
retire before it's light or you'll all be prisoners!'

Dawn was already breaking. Off we went, running like
hares through the bursting shells. This was one of the most
exciting moments of my life, breaking the record for the
hundred yards sprint. We were only just in time for the
Germans were only a few yards away from us. Before we

got away, the machine guns opened up like the devil. Luckily we only lost a few men and unfortunately a sack full of our mess provisions.

That night we noticed quite a few Germans prowling about just in front of our parapet. I've no idea what they were after. We scuppered about fifty and brought in two bodies to identify. It is very extraordinary, but the sight of them made me feel so sad – although they are such beasts. One, such a young, smiling, good-looking boy. He had a letter on him (one has to read them all) from his sweetheart, starting 'Darling Little Hans'. His death meant another broken heart and one could hardly help saying, '<u>What</u> is the use of it all?'

The next morning we retired behind the dam and then followed the most terrible morning I've ever experienced. We were holed up behind the bank, when the Boche got our range. Huge shells known as Black Marias were making a literally deafening noise and with holes fifteen feet across, each one giving off a cloud of thick black smoke as large as a <u>cottage</u>. Each shell killed or wounded ten to twenty men and <u>such</u> wounds. They were all crying out, screaming to be dressed, and we went around all morning binding up wounds with inadequately small bandages, not knowing which to help first.

You will never guess where <u>I</u> was hit a few minutes later – No, Mud, it was <u>not</u> the place that <u>you</u> were *thinking of! I never turn my back on the enemy! In fact it was the tip of my nose, which you have always laughed at for being so small. Anyway it only cut the skin and made everyone roar with laughter.*

I was just having my after-lunch Benson and Hedges when they attacked again. I could hear a Scottish regiment advancing in open order across a field to support us. They were under heavy fire but were still playing their pipes. I stood up to see them better and was immediately hit. The next thing I remember I was lying on my back in the trench with a terrible pain in my head. The adjutant (an awfully nice man) had put a bandage on it, but he was telling me I must make my way back to Boulogne as soon as possible or I would be taken prisoner. This was a frightening thought as we heard that one or two Canadian prisoners had recently been crucified.

I was helped out by my servant – a Scots boy called Hamish. For two hours he dragged me through fields and over ditches, sometimes crawling on all fours to evade snipers. By some happy chance, we found a dressing station. I was put in a car, then on a train, and finally here I am in the Rawalpindi hospital in Boulogne. Today I met the Padre who had buried dear George. He said he was too brave for his own good and always had his head and shoulders above the parapet. He was shot through the head and heart simultaneously and died instantly without pain.

I don't expect you to wade through all this, but I must pass the time somehow in bed. Now I must stop because I can hear the doctor coming. Lots of love to you and Gam-Gam.

Soon after he had recovered from his wounds, he went with his regiment to Salonica where he won the Military Cross for bravery, but was unable to forget the horror of the trenches, which haunted him for many years. He describes in his diary how he made one last attempt to banish the nightmares: 'I argued that if I drove down the Menin road in a Rolls Royce and smoked a cigarette on the dam of the Bellewaarde lake, sitting in the evening sun, with cattle munching the long grass and the sound of a reaper mowing – then how could I continue to dream of it as mud and stench?'

A much better solution lay in his next appointment as aide-de-camp to Lord French, Viceroy of Ireland. It was a change that affected the course of his life and left him no time for sad memories. Dick's new home was in Viceroy Lodge, Dublin, which Lord French shared with his voluptuous mistress, Wendy Bennett. Little did Dick realise, on being introduced to her, that he had just met his future mother-in-law.

Known to their friends as Peter Pan and Wendy, French and his mistress made an odd couple. She was six feet tall, and he hardly came up to her chin. Wendy had previously been married to a rather boring diplomat known as Pompous Percy, and had been only too happy to swap him for Peter Pan.

They met in 1915, when French was still in charge of the British Expeditionary Force. He wrote to her every week, describing troop movements and revealing future battle plans. If top people such as Churchill, Lloyd George or Kitchener came over for secret talks, he would pinpoint their meeting places and describe their itineraries in minute detail. These highly indiscreet letters, all signed Peter Pan, were delivered to Wendy by private equerry. One has the curious impression of a war being fought in Never Never Land.

In fact, he was unsuited to the job in every way. He hated the French, whom he accused of terrible atrocities, and he detested Kitchener, whom he described as useless and dangerous. 'However, my darling, with your gage in my hand and your love in my heart, there is no knightly thing I cannot do.' But the battle of Loos proved his final undoing. In his last letter to Wendy from the Front, he describes the terrible losses:

900 officers and 30,000 men, and that's only up to this morning. I shall be bearing the brunt of it, and it may even be a case of 'change the bowler'. Sometimes I wish

*they <u>would</u> send someone in to take my place, for I am
tired to death of this kind of life. War is such a very
brutal way of settling differences, and the more I see of
it, the more I hate it. Glory and her twin sister Murder.
I have had enough of them and all that matters to me
now is you, my darling Wendy. All my love as ever,
Peter Pan.*

Wendy had one daughter, Iris – my mother-to-be. Tall,
flat-chested, with long feet and striking violet eyes, she
thought of herself as a girl with two fathers, Pompous Percy
and Peter Pan. Peter, who always called her his 'darling
little Michael' (one of the Lost Boys), was still living happily with Wendy in Never Never Land. Percy, on the other
hand, was now British ambassador to Panama. Wendy had
had an exotic upbringing in Romania, in a family that still
greeted incoming guests with bread, salt and a five-gun
salute. Apparently she had been cared for by a gypsy wet-
nurse and had a tame bear that walked up and down on her
back if she was ill.

Keenly aware that her background meant she could
never be entirely accepted by English society, she made up
her mind that her daughter should become a pukka English
débutante and enjoy all the things that she had missed. Iris
was presented at Court, 'came out' and was soon all ready

to do the London Season. Life for the upper classes seemed
to be just one long party. Here is a typical week:

2 February Hair washed and curled, Selfridges. Lunch,
Ritz. Lord Leverhulme's Ball – get a man. Danced till
five thirty.

3 February Fitting for riding habit at Revency and
Rossiter. Lunch at The Chinese Restaurant. Saw
wonderful Russian ballet, *Cleopatra*, in Lady Cunard's
box with Lord Blandford.

4 February Rode in the Row, lunch at Ritz. Ball at Lady
de Lisle's. Wonderful evening. Danced with the P of W!!

5 February Shopping at Harrods. Opera cloak with
feathers, motoring bonnet, six pairs silk stockings.
Cosy afternoon with my darling friend Winks, eating,
talking, laughing, walking, criticising.

6 February Paraded in Park. Collected fancy dress,
Nathan's. Lunch at the Ritz. Three Arts Ball at Albert
Hall. Went as Galahad. Danced till three thirty.

7 February Nails manicured Selfridges, lunch Claridge's.
Thé dansant. Clara Butt. (A luke-warm affair.) Cinemah!

8 February General Strike. Rode home from the Bath
Club in a lorry. Great fun.

Clearly, Iris had no great interest in politics. Her diary
only mentions the war once, when two young soldiers
came to tea and told her heartrending stories about life in
the trenches. Her first reaction seemed almost one of
shocked surprise, as if war and its horrors were new to her.

Like all young people of that period, she was obsessed
with dancing. If new records arrived with the post, you
danced all morning. Then in the afternoon there was often
a *thé dansant*, and if you were unlucky and there was no ball
in the evening, there were two nightclubs you could go
to – the Grafton Galleries (very respectable) and Buzz
Buzz (if you were feeling naughty). One wonders what
gave them such manic energy as drink was never mentioned and Iris never admits to having a hangover.

The charleston had just come over from America but
somehow I cannot imagine my mother dancing it. I think
it was probably still the old-fashioned 'clutch 'n' glide' –
the foxtrot, the waltz and the tango. Apart from dancing,
they were also keen on what they called the 'Cinemah'.
Which, although the films were silent, was probably more
exciting than the theatre with its uninspiring play titles
such as *Joybells*, *Uncle Sam*, *Hello America*, and even *Oh,
Uncle!*. However, the first time Iris saw a serious play, *The*

Law Divine, she was so surprised and delighted that she went back twice.

Despite constant reminders in her diary to 'get a man', Iris had no boyfriend. Yet every day she was dining out at the Ritz, Claridge's or 'The Chinese Restaurant'. So although she had no regular date, there must have been no dearth of regular dinner partners, only too happy to share her table and foot the bill. No one thought of having a quick snack at home, any more than my mother would have dreamt of washing her own hair when she could have it done at Selfridges.

When peace was finally signed on 14 July, 1919, Iris was in Paris, staying with her Romanian relatives. Her aunt Sybille was the epitome of chic. She had a husband who looked like Maurice Chevalier and a white Pomeranian called Gigolo that she used to smuggle through Customs in her muff. The final signing of the treaty was celebrated in Paris with a grand review of troops. Iris, more thrilled by the peace than she had ever been by the war, watched in a state of patriotic fervour from her balcony: 'Some day!! Immense crowds had slept at the barricades all night. The English looked absolutely splendid as they marched down the street. It was the most stirring thing I have ever seen. Later there were fireworks and illuminations and the Eiffel Tower was lit from within by scarlet flames.'

On her last day, Iris went shopping and found the Parisian shops much better than those in London. She bought herself tortoiseshell opera glasses, an Onoto fountain pen, an evening cape with feathers, a motoring cloak and bonnet, and a gold wreath for her hair. Aunt Sybille gave her a beautiful blue fox fur with a blue Persian kitten to match. Iris's Paris diary ends on a truly Gallic note: 'Dined at the Ritz. Ate frogs.'

Iris returned to London to find a letter from Peter Pan waiting for her. 'Darling little Michael,' he wrote, using her pet name, 'we are both missing you terribly. Could you not somehow arrange for a little visit soon?'

It was a plea that Iris couldn't resist and in two weeks' time she was packing for Ireland. Knowing what to expect there, she put in two essential items: a smart evening dress and a pair of galoshes. She had a smooth passage – ('kitten as good as gold') – and was soon happily reunited with Peter and her mother. Unfortunately she was less happy with life at the Lodge.

Sunday, 3 August The formality of this place gives me the blues. When Peter comes into a room, we all have to bow or curtsy. Exploring the garden, I found detectives lurking behind every bush and the Chief

Senator was shot at the other day for not giving the right passwords.

Next day he came to lunch with us with his enormous wife. Very dull. Played Baccarat. Won tuppence.

Tuesday Soirée at Lady Headforte's. After dinner she sang comic songs while we all sat around yawning.

Wednesday Those foolish Ffolliots came to lunch. They prowled around like two old ducks quacking and then departed with the most affected farewell I've ever seen.

Thursday 5th Servants' Ball. Great fun. Danced with the Butler! (Best evening yet.)

Peter and Wendy were not having much fun either. Occasionally they managed to sneak incognito into town with Wendy heavily disguised and in a constant blue funk. Luckily Peter owned a little cottage, not far from Dublin, where he and Wendy could go to be alone. Iris also loved to stay there too, and discovered a whole new world of country pleasures, unknown to her in London. On one typical day, she 'fed pigs with a bottle, rode a donkey, milked cows, sang opera and danced on the Downs, went fishing but only caught a slug, taught the kitten to climb trees. A glorious day with every sense satisfied!' On rainy days, she stayed peacefully at home, knitting a jumper, writing poetry and playing with the kitten.

Wendy made one attempt to socialise with the neighbours, but it was not a success. 'Rowdy party at the Stewart-Browns,' Iris wrote. 'Florence is a repulsive hooligan.' The experiment was not repeated, but it had whetted Wendy's appetite for social life, which she was missing. In fact, she was getting a bit bored with the countryside and when she heard that the Sultan of Kashmir was coming to visit the Lodge, she couldn't resist the temptation to join in the celebrations, so she and Iris returned to Dublin. Iris wrote in her diary:

> *Friday, 29 August* Lunch with Rajah of K. Cinemah with
> Lord Castlereagh and Lord Bective. Big reception later
> for the Rajah. Captain Dickie Wyndham, very
> persistent. Crawled to bed at five a.m.

> *Saturday* Races at Phoenix Park. Greatest fun. Backed
> three winners. Dickie Wyndham very attentive again!

It had been love at first sight. Dick was not a man to waste time, and when Iris returned to London she found a letter waiting for her.

My dear Miss Bennett – Iris (erase word not required),
I hope I haven't mispellt your name but you must admit it
really is a difficult one. I put it in the same category as
'Piccaddilly'! 'Iris' would be very much easier! (Dick's
bad spelling was famous!)

I hope you don't mind my writing to you, but I'd like
to know your mother's views on chaperones. Are you
allowed to go out to dinner and a dance with a respectable
young man like myself?

You mustn't remind me that I have only met you three
times. I like to feel that I have known you all my life.
Yours, Dick.

P.S. When I know you better, I think I might also call
you 'Laughing Eyes', for even when you are serious, you
have a delightful trick of laughing with your eyes only, which
I love. I also love your scent. It beats my hair lotion to blazes.

In fact, there was no need for a chaperone as Dick's
sister, Olivia, was living at 10 Belgrave Square, our family
home in London. Olivia was an eccentric lady. In five years'
time, she was to run away with a black lesbian actress and live
the rest of her life in Harlem. But now she seemed a perfectly ordinary upper-class girl devoted to show-jumping.
She took an instant shine to Iris, which meant that Dick now
had a safe-house where they could meet without scandal.
After a respectable little tea party with Olivia, they could

sneak away to dance at the Grafton Galleries, and exchange a chaste kiss in the taxi on the way home. Anything more would have been unthinkable. Unfortunately these days of happiness were not to last much longer, as Dick had to return to his regiment. A week before leaving, he came to a sudden decision, and soon there was a date in Iris's diary heavily circled with red: '*Saturday 15 November* Hurst Park. DICK PROPOSES TO ME!'

Of course, she accepted, much to the delight of her mother, who saw Dick as a real catch – a rich young man who had recently inherited Clouds from his cousin Perfoo, recently deceased in the war. It was, however, a place he rarely visited as he was stuck with his regiment in Portsmouth, where he had expected life to be pretty dull – but the opposite was the case:

I've been leading the gay life here since I came back. Dances, dinners etc. galore. People seem even more dancing mad here than in London but you have to be very careful not to do any steps that are not quite in fashion. They're rather stiff and sedate functions which make me feel that I want to rush into the centre of the room and do our Apache dance or something really exciting.

As it is, I can only work off my feelings on my partner's toes. As for the girls here, I've never struck a worse collection of clodhoppers in my life. Sometimes I disappear upstairs and have a good think about the great times we've had together. I think of that night when we danced at the Grafton Galleries, trailing balloons behind us and blowing trumpets in each other's ears, and you tried to make me put on a red moustache, but I was too vain to do it. How wonderful it will be when we are married and can do everything together. Goodnight, my Angel.

Dickie

Iris, however, alone in London, was having second thoughts. Dick was so much older and cleverer than she. Would he find her too young, too immature and silly? She had read no good books, knew nothing of classical music. Often in the company of his clever friends, she would find herself tongue-tied unable to communicate her thoughts. What could she do to seem more grown-up? Dick soon reassured her:

My Darling. Enjoy yourself, for these days of your childhood are the best of your life. I should never forgive myself if I took them away from you. Remain a child for a little bit longer – a 'sun child'. Above all, never think that I could laugh at you for not being clever enough. I love you just as you are. For me, you can't improve – you are perfect! Goodnight, darling and be a happy little sun child for my sake. Dickie

31

Only one thing was worrying him. Long before they had met, Iris had promised her father that she would come for a long stay in Panama where he was now ambassador. As the dreaded date approached, Dick became more and more distraught, and his letters to Iris more frequent and depressing:

My Darling, I only wish I could enjoy the present without thinking of the future. I have always been the same; when I was a boy, as soon as the holidays began, I used to start worrying about having to go back to school. I'm afraid I'm rather a coward really: I hate suffering, not so much of the body but of the mind, and the thought of your departure is torturing me.

By now, Iris was quite looking forward to her trip, and all this whingeing was starting to get on her nerves. Being a sensible girl, she wrote with a suggestion that she thought might cheer him up. 'Wouldn't it be a good idea if we got married now, as soon as possible, instead of waiting all that time until I come back from Panama?'

Dick's reply to this was a classic combination of wise counsel with a hint of sheer panic:

I'm afraid this is going to be rather a pompous letter. First of all, I want you to realise that marriage is the biggest thing in one's life, especially for a girl. Once it's done, it's done; there is no going back. If it is a success, it means your life is a success, and if it fails, so does your life. Taking a husband isn't like engaging a servant or buying a horse. You can get rid of them. Yet some foolish people spend weeks engaging a butler, yet marry an acquaintance of a few days' standing at the Registry Office. Before we marry we have got to find out everything about each other, know each other as well as we know ourselves. It's madness to marry first, trusting to luck. You might as well buy a car because the paint is pretty. I was determined not to ask you to marry me for at least a year. I wanted to be free for a little longer, 'sow my wild oats', but I wasn't strong enough to wait and thank God I didn't. I knew that I loved you more than all the other girls rolled into one. I couldn't bear the thought that you might meet some other man and marry him without ever having known how much I loved you.

I want you to look on this engagement as a kind of apprenticeship. You mustn't let it hamper you in any way. Remember I am the first man you have really known. There are many many more – far nicer than me. I want you to meet them and get to know them, enjoy yourself – have your fling – and if one day you find you have made a mistake just write and say so – I shall understand. But in the meantime keep this engagement secret, so if you do *change your mind, no nasty people can say you have treated me badly, or any rot of that sort. In the meantime we'll see all we can of each other. As you said yourself, you don't really know me yet nor I you. (You mustn't marry and then find that I bore you when it is too late.) Also your shyness must go – your little shell must be broken. Then at the end of our apprenticeship, we can marry, knowing that like the prince and princess in the fairy stories, we shall 'live happily ever afterwards'.*

    I send you all my love,
    Dickie.

Whatever his views on marriage, Dick was certainly determined on one thing. Before leaving England, Iris must visit Clouds and see her future home. He had finally quit his regiment, and had returned to Clouds to rediscover the pleasures of being a country gentleman.

I have just got back from hunting, had a huge hot bath and huger tea!!! and am now enjoying that delicious tired comfortable feeling which can only really be induced by exercise, cleanliness and a full stomach. From the point of view of hunting, the day was not successful but I love it all the same. To be out all day in brown woods and green fields – on a horse. That is my idea of heaven. As that sometimes witty but always vulgar paper the

Pink 'Un *says, 'Paradise is only found on the back of*
a horse or in the arms of one's beloved.' Thank God you
will be coming here soon, so that we can enjoy a few last
days of Paradise together.

I wonder if you will love this countryside as I do. I
sometimes think it is even more beautiful now than in
the summer. I adore the bare trees with their spidery
twigs against the light grey sky, the brown leaves
underneath, the rain so fine and gentle that it is almost
mist and the distant hills, fading until they are lost in the
clouds. Soon you will be here, Darling, to share these
scenes with me.

Dick met Iris in full hunting costume and showed her
round the grounds and stables. She found it all very beautiful and impressive and later explored the house with
Olivia:

Never seen so many passages and rooms in my life.
Quite bewildering. It's really a lovely house – Dickie
must be proud of it. Later all the men went hunting
and I made friends with Olivia's tiny Shetland pony.
There were also lots of activities. We played golf, ping-
pong and badminton and danced after dinner to the
gramophone.

What happened next was a bit of a mystery. Iris was a dedicated diarist and for over a year she had not missed a single day. Suddenly, ten days are left blank – what could it have been that she found too trivial or too embarrassing to record? Did she catch a bad cold, fall off her horse, or have a dreadful row with Dickie? Or could it have been something rather more exciting? Alone together for the first time in their future home, there was now no reason for stolen kisses behind the summer-house at Belgrave Square. But of course they would never have gone beyond warm cuddles and tender caresses for Dick knew the rules and would never have broken them. But it must have been better than the summer-house.

Soon after her stay at Clouds, after a tearful goodbye, Iris, with Wendy as chaperone, boarded the *Patuca* for Jamaica – first stop before Panama.

At first, Dick bore up surprisingly well. He had not yet realised that letters took six weeks to arrive. Soon he began to feel as if he was writing into a void: 'It is the absolute powerlessness that is driving me mad,' he wrote. 'It almost seems that you are dead – that you can't exist – that you are just a dream. All I can say is, "Come back! Come back!" I must have you, Darling. This separation's even worse than I ever expected.'

He tried to bring the dream back to life – re-creating her through memories of happy days:

Such a glorious, sunny day, with great white and purple clouds blowing across the sky, casting shadows on the Downs – 'Our weather'. I took the same ride that we took together. I could see your darling face laughing in the wind and your hair breaking away from the last pins. And sometimes when it is cold, I can see you – your two beautiful eyes peering at me out of a great fur collar and I can feel your little fist clenched inside mine. Why do I torture myself with these memories? It's like when you have a dull toothache and you bite on it to make the pain sharper.

On board the *Patuca*, Iris kept her diary as usual.

6 January 1920 Horrible small boat, smelly and badly painted. Tiny cabin. Felt thoroughly miserable – and to think that only last night I was dining with Dickie at the Ritz! The other passengers are an extraordinary assortment, but very friendly. There is Madame Galinet – divorcée; Miss Ashton – sour spinster; Mr Mackay – drunken Scottie. Miss Moraes – Jamaican Jewess. Major Seymour – young man with decided but narrow views. Mr Fraser. Chi-chi? Miss Andrews – nice girl. Major Tulloch – verbose idiot. Lord Williams – very posh.

Saturday Marconi just came through to say a cyclone is reported near the Azores and we're running straight into it. Sat in the Saloon and listened to the wind rising to a scream in the rigging. Horrible night, thought my end had come. The boat began to pitch and roll, every timber creaked and sighed. The French woman tried to drown the noise by playing Indian love lyrics until the piano began to hit her in the face. Mummy asked me how long my lifeline was! She's now in her bunk and intends to remain there. The Captain says that he has only twice in a hundred voyages known it to be so rough for so long a time.

Wednesday Today the wind dropped a bit, so we all managed mutton chops for breakfast. Then Miss Andrews and I sat on the top deck and had a long conversation about re-incarnation.

Friday Fine hot day. Mrs Ashton in full tropical gear (with her petticoat hanging down behind). Miss Shaw got out her cotton stockings and we all felt very summery. Saw my first flying fish and won a bottle of champagne at Deck Tennis. The Captain persuaded me to try some of it and it made me feel so happy that I wrote a very nice letter to darling Dickie. After dinner I went up to the top deck. It was a glorious starlit night. I drank lemonade, smoked and thought many big thoughts. We are all getting to know each other much better now and all the strain is wearing off. The only person we avoid is the alcoholic Scotchman who has begun making very personal remarks.

Tuesday First sight of land for fifteen days. Haiti, a barren desolate shore with no sign of life or habitation, but I did see one perfect blue bay, ringed with golden sand.

Thursday 22 January Jamaica at last! A beautiful undulating island. Soft lights on the hilltops. Deep shadows in the gullies. We packed and dressed ready for 'shore going'. Miss Kent surpassed herself by appearing in a huge hat with ostrich plumes.

As we approached Port Royale the sea was suddenly full of woolly black heads, little Negro boys circling the boat like tadpoles and diving beautifully for pennies. Papa sent a car for us, but what a ride! The road was full of potholes and teeming with brightly dressed black people giving off a strong, very strong coconutty smell! Now, thank goodness, I'm sitting at last at an open window overlooking the sea, a cool breeze coming off the water, listening to a Negro band playing 'A Perfect Day'. The nights here are extraordinary. They seem to get into one's blood. One feels the allure, the passionate message of the Tropics. Anything seems possible here. The atmosphere is so sensuous, with the brilliant stars above and the hot still air draining away your vitality. Everyone is so kind. They can't do enough for us. They've given us our own little house and we get breakfast in bed.

Saturday Went for a lovely drive past the Blue Lagoon and funny little Negro villages. I just lay back and let the atmosphere soak into me. It was dark when we got back and the fireflies came out and settled in my hair.

Monday 4 p.m. Board the Santa Mater, a dirty American boat with rotten food, for a rough, hot, smelly, nauseating journey across the Caribbean sea. Arrive in Panama three hours early – no Papa in sight, only a dirty-looking dago who we used as a porter, only finding out too late that he was in fact the governor of Colon. Papa turns up, perspiring and angry, all his arrangements having gone wrong. We are jolted across the Isthmus in a special train, which reduces us to bruised jellies. They told us that every sleeper in this railway had cost a life from Yellow Fever. Directly we arrived all the staff – both black and white – rushed to greet us with bouquets flying, and there was even a presidential carriage with prancing horses to take us to our hotel – all most amusing! What fun!

But her euphoria didn't last for long. Iris soon realised that life at the embassy was just an endless round of receptions, dinners and dances, the same boring London scene all over again but this time without any friends to laugh with.

I have discovered why everything is such an effort here including the dances and dinner parties. It is because there is not a soul with whom I have anything in common. I'm isolated among a crowd, who look at things from an entirely different point of view – who seem in fact to be speaking an entirely different language. The American colony are the worst, I think. They are refined scandalmongers, always prying into people's affairs and then picking them to pieces. (They also say rude things like 'there goes that bum Gallagher'. I know everyone says it now but I just can't get used to hearing 'that word'!) They think that I am a little mad, I believe. Luckily, I have one good ally here, apart from Judge Hannan, and that is Captain Zerbee who runs the local riding stables. He takes me for wonderful morning gallops across the Savannah and yesterday we visited my first tropical jungle! I saw orchids and spider lilies, hummingbirds and monkeys, and there was this hot, heavy jungle scent that went straight to my head. Then, after an hour's riding we reached Chirico Pool, emerald green water shadowed by great trees. The lizards run across it on their tails! It was so cool and quiet there, the first peace I had felt since I came to this sun-soaked country.

On the other hand, I'm a bit worried about Zerbee. I've often noticed him staring at me lately with unconcealed admiration; the other day, a member of the American 'Cats Corner' whispered to me, 'I think Mr Zerbee has got a case on you.' Could she be right? I'd better tell him about Dickie right away.

16 March Lord Williams, who loves to go riding with us, nearly got eaten by a crocodile yesterday. Zerbee had tethered our horses to the trees by the pool, and we were watching two black snouts, snapping and grunting, when Lord Williams heard a hissing noise just behind him. He turned round and saw to his horror the snout of a nine-foot crocodile protruding from a bush only three feet away from his legs. Luckily he had a gun with him and shot the crocodile through the head. The terrified horses broke their bridles and raced away into the jungle, so we had to walk all the way home. Lord Williams spent the whole trip back talking to me about the subconscious mind. Very boring!

Carnival time Everyone wearing their best 'polleras' and dancing the Tamberito, a graceful gliding dance to flutes and tom-toms. We went to a moonlit dance in a banana grove. Hundreds of coloured lights, full moon and everyone in white and gold. It was like fairyland. Everyone was dancing the Tamberito and Mr Hughes and I were persuaded to enter the ring. There was wild applause and roars of laughter as neither of us had the vaguest idea of the real steps. However, we pranced about whilst my mother wrung her hands in an agony of embarrassment.

Next morning the local press went to town on us. 'Iris Bennett, one of the most radiantly good-looking women to have ever come to the Isthmus, the admiration of all at the Tamberitos. Not one soul would not look with admiration at so beautiful an incarnation of Youth. One of England's fairest flowers, she has already made a sensation.'

7 *March* At last a letter from Darling Dickie. After six weeks. I have not let it go all day.

Of course I have told Zerbee about Dick, and how we hope to get married soon, but he shows no signs of adjusting himself as promised. He sits and looks at me and tells me wonderful things about myself, and I sit and listen and just feel very sad for him. He understands the situation absolutely yet he goes straight ahead. The pleasure he gets now he thinks will balance the pain he will feel when I am gone. Rather cruelly, I showed him the letter from Dickie and left him looking very thoughtful and very hard hit.

Great excitement! The Prince of Wales is coming to visit Panama and Pa is giving a ball in his honour. All the high society ladies have dashed out to buy new ball gowns just in case he should ask them to dance. They have also decided that the exaggerated court bow is too formal so the old-fashioned colonial curtsy is back in favour.

Next problem was how to address him – what was his correct title. 'Waal,' said Miss Peebles, 'I don't know about you girls but I'm going to call him Sweetie.'

A big crowd turned out to greet him, all singing his praises. 'Isn't he a splendid wholesome looking boy?' cried one lady. 'Every inch a man!' One paper described him as being 'in the pink of condition, clear blue eyes and a face that glowed with health – more like eighteen than twenty-five'. There were a few who objected to his easy and democratic manner and what they called his obvious predilection to be 'one of the boys', unsuitable in a future king. In order to make him appear more regal, they gave him a smart military escort. One little boy, seeing their brilliantly coloured uniforms, ran home and told his mother that he had just seen the Prince of Wales with all of the men from the circus with him.

Pa's dance itself was a great success though a good many people nearly burst themselves with envy, as the Prince didn't dance with anyone he should have danced with. Instead he led off with me. And after a couple of dances, I noticed him making eyes at a pretty little girl in black satin and ostrich plumes. She was called Miss Cranberry and the Prince spent most of the evening dancing with her. Finally, Miss Lefevre who had organised the ball could stand no more and whispered violently in the august ear, 'She's the boilermaker's daughter and has not been invited,' but the Prince obviously did not give a hoot and went on dancing.

However, Miss Lefevre was determined to have her innings at any cost and she came up to the Prince and announced that she wanted to introduce him to some of the 'flowers of Panama'! Whereupon the flowers were paraded forth, one darker than the other. The Prince shook hands with them but didn't ask a single one to dance. Instead he backed towards me and whispered, 'For God's sake get me out of this.' I sneaked him quietly onto the verandah whereupon he sat mopping his brow and declaring himself 'all in'.

'But aren't you going to dance with any of those ladies – I thought Rita was quite pretty?' I asked him. 'What! The black one! Not for this little boy!' After that we sat smoking and having fun but couldn't find a drink. Finally the Prince spotted a little Jamaican waiter who brought him a whiskey and soda. The Prince was so delighted that he shook hands with the waiter who immediately burst into tears of joy.

Next morning the papers were full of 'the Cranberry Scandal':

According to Miss Cranberry, the prince is 'just crazy about American jazz music. As for his dancing, he is quite good at the foxtrot and the waltz but as a one-stepper he's divine!' Our reporter at the ball last night, although maybe a little confused by the chemical reaction produced internally by a mixture of Brut extra dry and whiskey, nevertheless reports that he saw the Prince stalking the ballroom with a 'come-to-sweetie' expression on his face until the presentation was accomplished.

Soon after, when all the excitement had died down, Miss Cranberry was offered a film contract and the Prince left for England. Now, all that was left to us to remind us of the glamour and excitement of the past few days was a notice on a billboard announcing a 'Closing Sale, with everything going cheap on account of "no further use". Fine fancy-dress ball gowns, silk stocking, the finest face paint and powder, switches, wigs, false teeth and dance pumps. Contact the Sec. Canal Zone Elite Society'.

But Iris had thoughts only for the future.

8 April Only two days to go before I board the Megantic for England! On the last night, my little maid Ramona came to say goodbye and brought her pet monkey with her, the loveliest monkey ever seen with little black fingers that clung round my arm. I think she's very sorry to see me go. Afterwards, I sat on the verandah watching the sunset, and the beauty of it almost hurt me. Of course, I'm longing for England and Dickie but nevertheless I think I shall miss Panama quite a lot.

10 April Board the Megantic. Found a boat letter waiting for us. Judge Hannan who had been a great admirer of me and Mum. It was very long and exceedingly pompous. 'In all my experience, I have never met a more intelligent, wise, noble, sincere and true Mother and Daughter. Your sweet influence has

47

left behind rays of sunshine to assist us along Life's journey towards a higher and nobler purpose.' Much more to the point was a Marconigram from Zerbee. 'Much love pet. Missing you sadly, Zerb.' My fellow passengers here are mainly Australian and very cordial. I have made two good friends, Tootles and 'Bulgy' Thorne. We are known as the Clan. There is also one maddening little boy simply known as 'the Nuisance'. There has only been one row as yet, when Colonel Thorne threatened to throw a German overboard for attempting to walk off with our deck chairs.

29 April England in sight! Cooler weather at last. Now I can put powder on my nose without it turning into a sticky white plaster.

30 April Home at last! But met by Olivia with bad news. Darling Dickie has had an accident riding in a steeplechase and broken his nose.

10 May Dickie recovering. Our engagement has been announced. Dickie, determined not to lose me again, has started to make plans for our wedding.

Iris, of course, was thrilled to bits but she couldn't help feeling rather nervous. It had all happened so quickly and she knew so little about what lay ahead. The obvious person to ask for advice was her mother. Shortly before the big day she crept up to the bedroom where Wendy was already fast asleep in her curlers, with a chin strap tied on top of her head. She was in no mood to be woken but Iris persisted.

'Mummy,' she said, 'I'm sorry to bother you like this but I must have your advice. What do I have to do to please a man?'

Wendy, clearly not in the mood for a heart-to-heart or embarrassing details, was brief: 'Well, darling. Remember to always use lots of scent and never let him see you brush your teeth.' And that was it. A week later Iris, armed with no further advice, married Dick at Christchurch, Lancaster Gate on 20 October, 1920, with the Bishop of Salisbury officiating.

She wore a gown of soft white satin with a panel of silver embroidery on the skirt and a long train. 'One of the loveliest brides I have ever seen,' gushed Mrs Gossip in her society column. 'Viscount French attended, wearing a top hat that made him look considerably taller.' The Prince of Wales, who could not attend, gave Iris a beautiful diamond brooch.

Afterwards Wendy hosted a big reception and received her guests standing regally at the top of the stairway in a gown of grey charmeuse and a hat of flame-coloured velvet. Iris, dancing happily with Dick, thought it the best day of her life.

After the last guests had left, Dick drove his new bride to the Ritz for the first night of their honeymoon. This was the moment Iris had been dreading, not so much the love-making – Dick would surely know how to take care of that – but the fear that in her ignorance she might do the wrong thing and look foolish. She had no idea that Dick, although he was now twenty-six, was also still a virgin and hadn't the slightest idea how It was done. In his desperate attempts to find out, he caused Iris terrible pain, but achieved nothing. My mother, who once described her experience to me, said that it had been quite terrifying: she had felt as if she were being torn apart. When they woke in the morning, they could hardly bear to look at each other – Iris full of pain and frustration, Dick crippled by embarrassment and shame. Sadly, as they felt there was no point in trying again, they drove to the nearest doctor, who penetrated her hymen with a surgical instrument. As a result, my mother was frigid for life. 'Did you know,' she once asked a friend, 'that women also have their moments, just like men do? I wonder what it feels like.' But my poor mother was never to find out.

Fortunately, Dick still loved her, though perhaps in a different way. She would need all the love and support she could find to cope with what came next.

Only just out of her teens, and accustomed to a life of non-stop dancing and pleasure, Iris suddenly found herself mistress of Clouds. She was now responsible for the upkeep of a huge country house and its servants. There was a butler, a housekeeper, a cook and a footman, plus assorted housemaids, kitchen-maids and laundry-maids. There were also grooms, gardeners and someone who was mysteriously known as the Odd Boy, a youngster who did all the unpopular jobs shunned by the higher-ranking staff.

Dick soon realised that this huge staff was unnecessary, and reduced it by more than half. But there was still a butler on a hundred pounds a year, a housekeeper on fifty, a cook on forty and assorted underlings on thirty-five, but nothing for the Odd Boy, who presumably was happy with a pat on the head and a bag of humbugs.

It was important for her to remember that all the men must be addressed by their surnames, although the women were quite happy to be Kate, Sally or Doris. The exception was the housekeeper, who must always be addressed respectfully by her surname.

Iris, who could barely add two and two together, was now responsible for the wages book and also for keeping the household accounts. The dreaded list began with 'Baker, Butcher, Butterman and Chandler' and ended with 'Beer' – the biggest item of all since the servants drank nothing else. She sometimes found herself envying the housemaids – she could easily have learnt to scrub a floor – but anything to do with figures was beyond her.

Dick was enjoying life enormously. While Iris toiled away at her household chores, he was out in the open air doing all the things he loved best – hunting, fishing, coursing, riding at point-to-points, or racing round the countryside in his open-topped silver Rolls Royce. He also enjoyed weekend entertaining, and Iris was responsible for sending out the invitations and checking the acceptances. Then she had to interview the housekeeper, the formidable Miss Bishop, to make sure there was an adequate supply of clean sheets and towels, doilies and napkins, fresh flowers in every room, a sufficient supply of matches distributed throughout the house for the convenience of pipe-smokers. Next the cook had to be consulted, to make sure that nothing unpopular was going to be on the menu, and finally the butler, who kept the key to the silver cupboard. Everything needed had to be taken out and polished: egg spoons, marrow spoons, coffee spoons, dessert knives and oyster forks, menu-card holders, napkin rings and silver baskets.

Weekend parties were quite strenuous, with tennis, badminton and Crazy Croquet, followed by dancing in the evenings. Iris was often too tired to enjoy them but she was a gutsy girl, determined not to let darling Dickie down.

She made a list in her diary:

THINGS I MUST REMEMBER TO DO TO KEEP FIT AND WELL AND HAPPY.

I. Sleep with windows wide open.

2. Tepid baths – do not stay long in a hot one.

3. <u>Always</u> get up for breakfast and if possible take a short walk before it.

4. Try not to eat too fast or too much.

5. Not to smoke too much.

6. Try to bring my mind more to bear on household matters!?

7. Always have an <u>occupation</u>. <u>Never</u> be lazy.

8. Always be unselfish.

9. Try and be more observant with names and faces especially guests and servants.

10. Try to improve my mind regarding natural history etc.

11. Remember to call meal in middle of day <u>Luncheon!!</u>

As if all this were not enough she went on to make lists of all the things her family liked or didn't like to eat, later to be sent to the cook. Dick's list was the longest.

<u>He likes</u> – crab, oysters, jugged hare, bread sauce, porridge and strong China tea. He does <u>not</u> like – treacle pudding, toasted cheese or fried eggs.

<u>I</u> like cottage pie and chocolate pudding but draw the line at Mulligatawny soup and undercooked steak.

<u>Olivia</u> hates macaroni cheese and boiled cod.

<u>Grandpa Guy</u> is easiest of all. He just hates parsnips.

Of course there was the occasional excitement – hunt ball and dances given by Lady Pembroke at Wilton House or the Baths at Longleat. She also enjoyed shopping trips to London, which she combined with having her hair permed or going to 'the movies' – the new smart word, which had now replaced 'Cinemah' in her vocabulary. Her shopping needs, of course, varied with the seasons. In winter it might be a white rabbit-skin wrap with matching muff; in summer, a fan, a sunbonnet, a bathing costume.

But a new interest was about to come into her life. The village Brownies were looking for a new Brown Owl (unfortunately known as the BO). Iris let it be known in the village that she might be interested, and one summer's morning she opened the garden door to find them all lined up on her lawn: Doris, Alice, Rose, Elsie, Joy, Irene and Winnie, all dressed in their smartest Brownie outfits.

They took one step forward and burst into the Brownies' war cry:

We're the Brownies
Here's our aim
Lend a hand
And play the game.
La-la-la!

At first Iris was taken aback by this sudden intrusion and felt like beating a hasty retreat, but after a while she found that she couldn't resist so many cheerful smiles and decided to test them further. The first thing, surely, was to find out how genuine they were, so she asked Winnie, who appeared bossy enough to be their leader, whether she could recite the Brownie law. Winnie needed no prompting and even stood at attention: 'A Brownie's honour is to be trusted. A Brownie is a friend to all and a sister to every other Brownie no matter what social class they belong to. A Brownie is courteous, a friend to animals, obeys the Brownie law, smiles and sings under all difficulties, is thrifty, pure in thoughts, words and deeds.' As Winnie finished, with a smart salute, Iris noticed that all the other girls were now looking towards her, their eyes full of expectation. She realised that, like it or not, she was now their newly elected BO.

But now that she had them, what on earth was she going to do with them? Luckily she found something called *The Brownies' Handbook*, which gave her a few hints.

Exercises, for instance, sounded like a good way to start the ball rolling. There was tiptoe-marching, jumping up and down on the spot, leg- and arm-swinging, frog-hopping and something mysterious called Giants and Dwarfs. She was also glad to discover that, should it rain, she could take them indoors and teach them to pick up hankies with their teeth.

Over the next few weeks, Iris became increasingly fond of her Brownies and soon found herself frog-hopping happily around the lawn with the best of them. She wrote little plays for them to perform, usually based on nursery rhymes – 'A Little Nut Tree', 'Ride-a-Cock-Horse' and 'Three Blind Mice'. They sang and danced and played violently competitive games – French and English, or Fox and Geese – and there were prizes for the Brownie with the cleanest nails and the smartest uniform.

Dick, too, had discovered a new interest in life. As a boy he had been fond of sketching but now, inspired by the beauty of the countryside around him, he had decided to try his hand at painting. He was encouraged in this by the Vorticist artist Wyndham Lewis, an unscrupulous character who saw in Dick a prospective patron. He offered to teach him to paint and Dick happily agreed. The lessons proved helpful and Dick had no objection to paying for them, but soon discovered that Lewis expected a great deal more from him than that. He found to his surprise that a lot of his friends, including the Sitwells, were giving Lewis money on a regular basis and he reluctantly agreed to follow their example.

When the upkeep of Clouds proved a terrible drain on his finances, and his payments started to peter out, furious letters arrived – 'Where's my fucking stipend, eh, Dick?' Dick ignored them and Lewis plotted his revenge. In *The Apes of God*, a vitriolic book devoted to making fun of artists other than himself, he describes Dick as 'the world's prize ape – a typical Champagne Bohemian – one who likes to work in filthy paint-stained overalls whilst chewing the stem of a well-seasoned briar before ordering his lunch-eon from Fortnum and Mason's. He is conceited, foolish, a clumsy mover and great farter – who lives in a glass vacuum where his own image is reflected from every wall.' But Dick took it in his stride. He was far too happy, painting at Clouds, to worry about his friend's treachery.

As for Iris, she had recently found herself getting plumper – no bad thing, as she had always hated her flat chest, and she also noticed that those nasty messy affairs that used to happen every month had recently stopped. Even so it came as quite a shock to her when, on a routine visit to the local doctor, she discovered that she was nearly three months pregnant.

She was thrilled at the news and only hoped that Dickie would feel the same way. He certainly looked pleased enough, but it was for one reason only: his desperate need for an heir to inherit Clouds, which might otherwise pass into alien hands. During the next few months, Iris was astonished at the care Dick lavished on her: he made sure she ate nourishing foods, rested properly and kept out of the sun. She sometimes wondered what all the fuss was about, as she had no worries about her pregnancy: she simply assumed that everything was bound to be all right. She was also too vague to keep a proper account of the months – I was forced occasionally to give her a smart kick, to remind her that somebody was in there, longing to get out.

One day in early October, Dick went off to ride in the local point-to-point. Iris, at home, knew she was supposed to rest but couldn't bear the thought of a whole day without him. After a quick flick of *papier poudré* on her nose, and a dab of lipstick (more was considered common), she was off driving her little red Austin Seven at its usual breakneck thirty miles an hour. Reaching the racecourse, she positioned herself as near as possible to the rails.

Predictably, Dick fell at the third fence and Iris, with a loud scream, clapped her hands to her eyes. Inside her, two little pink buds were raised in sympathy. The horse was killed but Dick survived with a few bruises, and five hours later, I was born with my hands still over my eyes. Dick went through all the right motions, congratulated my mother and gave me a little kiss but inside he was muttering to himself, 'Christ, it's a girl!' Iris sensed his disappointment and knew its cause, but naturally hoped that as I grew older he would learn to love me. Unfortunately my mother's Baby's Progress Book, kept over a number of years, made this seem unlikely: 'Joan,' she wrote, 'bites her nails, dribbles incessantly, is clumsy, obstinate and contrary. Has terrible yelling fits and fidgets all the time, cracking her joints, picking her nose, and making strange sizzling noises.' No wonder Dick avoided the nursery like the plague.

He started to spend most of his time in London with his 'Champagne Bohemian' friends, which left Iris, who had hired a nanny for me, free to plan Christmas. Apart from a hundred and fifty small toys for village children, she also had to find thirty or forty presents for friends and relatives. Luckily, her mother had been brought up in Romania, and had taught her the word '*scatta*' – Transylvanian for a small dog turd but used to describe cheap, unexciting or sometimes useless gifts, often second hand or hand-made. 'Terribly sorry, Lady Pembroke, I'm afraid it's only a *scatta*,' you murmur apologetically, as you watch her unwrap a hand-knitted egg cosy.

My mother's Christmas list started with one or two really nice presents for close relatives, but after that it was '*scattas*' for everyone. Among the most popular were pencil-boxes, table-runners, matchboxes, coat-hangers, bedsocks, blotting-paper, lavender bags, eyeglass cleaners, bookmarks, tea-cosies, hot-water-bottle covers, sponge-bags, kettle-holders and pin-cushions. My mother also made a short list of presents that she would like to be given: 'Brownie camera, silk bloomers, and a statue of the Sacred Heart'.

Meanwhile, Dick was still whooping it up in London with a group of smart new friends, among them his favourite, Irene, Marchioness of Queensberry. She returned his affection but nevertheless found his behaviour rather puzzling. Although evidently he liked her quite a lot, he had never suggested going to bed with her, as all her previous partners had. She had no way of knowing that, after his disastrous honeymoon, his interest in sex had dwindled almost to nothing. Irene, who knew herself to be a beautiful and attractive woman, found his attitude positively insulting and soon she was finding pretexts not to see him. Dick was reluctant to lose their friendship, and decided in the end to give her what she apparently wanted – after all, it was not a thing of any importance. He soon found out how wrong he'd been: his first experience of a truly orgasmic woman was more wonderful than anything he'd ever dreamt of. Naturally it had a profound effect on him, and in his excitement he foolishly mistook it for love.

When he got home he found Iris finishing her list of Christmas invitations. 'I see you haven't got the Queensberrys down,' he said, peering over her shoulder. 'They're a bit grand but awfully good fun.' Iris, always happy to oblige him, wrote down the names of Irene and her husband.

Christmas Day came and was a huge success, with crackers, balloons, a Christmas tree ablaze with wax candles and Dick dressed as Santa Claus with a sack of *scattas*. Dinner was turkey with all the trimmings and afterwards there was dancing. True to tradition, Dick had reserved the first two dances for Iris, but later she noticed him spending rather a lot of time on the floor with Irene, even partnering her in the last waltz. At two in the morning, after everyone else had gone to bed, Iris had a sudden moment of anxiety. Had all the candles on the Christmas tree been put out? She remembered the story of the ashes in the cupboard and how Clouds had gone up in flames. She crept down quietly, snuffer in hand, and saw that the candles were still blazing, but behind the tree, she made out two shadowy figures. As she got nearer she realised, to her horror, that Dick and Irene were clasped in each other's arms, exchanging hungry kisses. They were far too absorbed in each other to notice her, so she made her escape as quickly as possible. She left the Christmas candles alight, but quite probably she wouldn't have minded if the house *had* burnt down – provided, of course, that Irene was in it.

For the next few days, Iris stayed quietly in her room and said nothing to Dickie of what she had seen. After all, what could a few kisses mean? But she soon noticed that Dick was visiting London far more often than he had in the past and only on the flimsiest pretexts. Sometimes he put down the phone hastily when she came into a room. One day, she decided to ignore her principles and listen at the door. As a result of what she heard, there was soon a date in her diary, heavily circled with black ink, the initials IQ – Irene Queensberry – written beside it.

Iris was now determined on a divorce, but before making any irrevocable decision, she sought the advice of Guy, her much loved and trusted father-in-law. His advice was a trial separation, but 'to keep up appearances' Dick should make the occasional visit to Clouds. Reluctantly Iris agreed. She was determined to be brave but when it came to the last goodbye she broke down and cried uncontrollably on Dick's shoulder. For Dick, already riddled with guilt, this was unbearable and he could not wait to depart. He wrote her a letter of explanation:

Darling Iris,

I left because I could not bear to hear you talking so sadly or to see you looking so unhappy and to know I am the cause of it. Nor could I bear to see you trying to kiss my hands when I am not worthy to kiss your boots.

We can always be great friends and I couldn't get on without you. So don't let us talk about it any more.

Dickie.

Faced with the prospect of the separation, Iris was determined to put a brave face on it. Her social life went on much as before: 'Ball at Longleat. Visit to Lady Pembroke – Joan held court. Jumble Sale at Women's Institute.' Only the Brownies were abandoned: bereft of their beloved BO, they were reduced to hemming handkerchiefs.

Iris also had me for company – a mixed blessing judging by the continued entries in the Baby's Progress Book.

Joan is never still for one moment and exhausts all who look after her. When finally tired out, she sits and twiddles her hair without ceasing.

Hearing Hears more than is good for her.

Smell Good, but has a habit of snorting.

Sight Slight squint.

Taste Greedy.

Not a very pretty picture! But, luckily for Iris, my nanny Jessie was there ready to take me off her hands. If I yelled too loudly, her advice was always to slap a bit of salt on my tongue – but my mother was too soft-hearted for such brutal treatment.

In fact, if left to herself, she would probably have coped quite well with the separation. It was Dick's occasional mandatory visits that upset her – the nightmare of those silent meals and separate bedrooms. To make matters worse, Dick sometimes had a change of heart and wrote her letters that gave her false hope. In one letter, he tells her: 'Irene and I have decided to make a real effort to end all this, and I'm sure that things must come right in the end. You, Father and Joan are the only stable things that I have left and I could not get on without you. It is only the devil in me that hurts you, so please, darling, just be patient for a little bit longer.'

It was letters like these that caused Iris, in a moment of

blind faith, to start redecorating my nursery. Then came the moment of truth.

My Darling Iris,

I'm afraid that I am still in love with Irene, and am still seeing her. We have tried three times to separate for good which was a mistake for it is only when I think that I am never going to see her again that I become quite insane and feel prepared to go to any lengths to hold on to her.

I realise what a wonderful wife you are and worthy of the greatest love a man can give — but love is not the gift of God, as they say, it is the weapon of the devil, and we have no control over it. I hate to think I am making you unhappy, but my God, I am suffering too, as I deserve to. I sometimes think I shall go mad. You mustn't blame Irene for all this. She has tried harder than I have to end it — but mankind is very weak, except for a few, who are inhuman. I sometimes wonder if anyone has a happy life? Your mother thinks that I am just playing about but she doesn't realise that I am going through a hell of my own making. I feel very old — let's be friends, darling, at all costs. Dick.

After that, divorce was inevitable. Iris claimed that they had been happy for fifteen months but after that Dick had ceased to care for her.

Needless to say, the Marchioness of Queensberry was far too grand to be cited as co-respondent and Dick, to save her blushes, was obliged to do the decent thing expected of him. This involved a visit to the Cavendish Hotel, whose owner, Rosa Lewis, was only too happy to procure a tart for him and a double room at the Hotel Metropole in Brighton where she kept a tame waiter. His job was to bring up the breakfast tray and later swear that he had seen them naked in bed together. Pompous Percy had obtained his divorce in the same way but, too embarrassed to undress, he had sat up all night fully clothed and only dived beneath the sheets at the last moment. Dick on the other hand probably enjoyed it all enormously. Iris, meantime, knowing that she must soon leave Clouds, was in a state of lonely despair. She had no idea where she would go or what she would do, and felt that her life had suddenly come to an end.

Then something happened that saved her sanity. She had a call from Sidonie Houselander, the artist who had been redecorating my nursery. Apparently there were still some finishing touches to be done – could Iris put her up for a couple of weeks? Iris agreed reluctantly, for there could hardly have been a more ill-assorted pair. Sid, as she was known, thought of Iris as a 'stuck-up little deb' and Iris had described Sidonie to her friends as 'an arty freak'. She was certainly an odd-looking creature, with bright red hair, horn-rimmed spectacles and a dead white face. She had always hated her naturally rosy cheeks and used thick white makeup to disguise them. She was also a chain-smoker with a cigarette perpetually dangling from one side of her mouth and a permanent brown stain running down to her chin.

She had been brought up by her terrifying mother, Gert, who rode a motorbike wearing a crash helmet and ran a boarding house for drop-outs and failures. Sid did all the cleaning and washing-up, but she finally managed to escape from Gert and went to art school.

The great love of her life had been Sydney Reilly, widely acknowledged to be the most accomplished spy of his generation working for MI6. With his consummate grasp of five languages, he was a master of disguise who revelled in his ability to pose successfully as a German officer in the Kaiser's army or as a member of the Communist élite in Soviet Russia. A recent biography, *Ace of Spies*, describes him as the original inspiration for Ian Fleming's James Bond. Sid told Iris she still dreamt about him, kept his photo by her bed and had been 'torn in shreds' by her feelings for him; she had even given up Catholicism while their affair had lasted.

Over the next few weeks she and Iris spent most of their time together and were surprised by how much they enjoyed each other's company. Sid, who found Iris adorable, did everything she could to cheer her up and soon, no longer lonely, Iris was even learning to laugh again.

Sid was genuinely fond of Iris, but she also had an ulterior motive: a fanatical Roman Catholic, she had spotted in her a potential convert to the true faith. 'If only you'd believe in the mercy and kindness of God,' she told Iris, 'you'd soon forget that wretched business with Dick and find happiness again.' It sounded like a wonderful proposition, and shortly afterwards, to Sid's delight, she agreed to be rebaptised. Her first confession, which followed, proved more difficult as she couldn't think of a single thing she'd done wrong – except for wishing that Irene would fall under a bus. Soon after that it was my turn to be dunked in the cold water of the font, yelling my head off and trying to bite the priest.

Now Dick made it plain to Iris that she must move out of Clouds: he had decided to let or even sell the place, which had become a useless and expensive burden to him.

Iris left as soon as she could, and we spent the next few years living in Wendover, a small village in the Chilterns. I was happy there as we had two goats, which we milked every morning, and later my mother had a goat cart made for me, which I drove up and down the high street, waving my little whip. However, she still pined for London and when Dick came up with some much-needed financial help, she was able to buy a house just off the Fulham Road – a friendly area with a Bohemian atmosphere and a joy to shop in.

Most of our provisions came from Cullen's grocery where Mr Cullen stood behind the counter in his spotless white coat, weighing everything on his silver scales. Wonderful cakes and tarts came from Mrs Deschuyter's Belgian *pâtisserie*. But my favourite shop of all was Tullys, where Iris went for her embroidery silks. Her money was put into a little silver tube that hurtled across the ceiling on a wire to a cashier who sent the change whizzing back.

At the far end of the Fulham Road were what we called the Fearful Four: St Stephen's Hospital, the Servite Church, Mr Buckley the undertaker, and the Brompton Cemetery. All you needed, in fact, to depart from this life with the minimum of fuss.

On the brighter side, we had the magnificent Forum Cinema, which gave you splendid value for one and ninepence. First the organist would rise slowly from the lower depths, brilliantly spotlit, his fingers already straying over the keys. Then the curtains would part for a song-and-dance act or some sort of competition, usually Yo-Yo or Biff-Bat. Only then could the cock crow for *Pathé Gazette* and the long-awaited double bill, usually one good film followed by a lousy one.

Our house was in Evelyn Gardens, a quiet square backed by a beautifully tended communal garden. Apart from my mother and me, there was also Wendy, my granny, left sad and lonely after the recent death of Peter Pan. She had received no sympathy from Pompous Percy, who had left Panama for Hove where he had married a rich widow called Mrs Mustard and become president of the local bowls association. The rest of our household consisted of my nanny Jessie, Winnie, the housemaid, and a jolly Irish cook called Kathleen, whose hair was constantly escaping from its pins. I used to love her steamed puddings until one night a couple of her hairpins turned up in the Spotted Dick. There was also Brady, the gardener, the only man I have ever known who cleaned his teeth with soot.

It was quite a jolly household and Iris missed Dick less and less. The person she did miss – rather to her surprise – was Sid, who had moved to London to live with her mother, but so far had not called on her. 'My dearest Sid,' Iris wrote, 'How can I thank you for all the love and care you gave to me when I was at my lowest ebb? You were like a hand held out to me in the dark, a source of light and warmth for my poor frozen heart. Let's meet again soon. You'll be glad to see how much happier I am.'

Soon Sid was visiting my mother regularly. Then one night she arrived carrying a small suitcase and never went home. My mother sent for her books and easel and created a small studio for her on the top floor. Sid showed her gratitude by decorating my nursery yet again with scenes from fairyland.

There were few cosier places than an old-fashioned nursery – a popping gas fire, with a ring for the kettle, and a big iron fender with towels drying on it. On one side of the fire was my sofa, conveniently next to a bookcase where I could lie all day, sucking oranges and reading fairy stories. On the other side, Nanny sewed or knitted, with her dog Lucky at her feet in his malodorous basket. To complete my pleasure, there was my Victorian rocking-horse from Clouds and a large dressing-up box, so well stocked that one day I could be the Fairy Queen and the next day Hiawatha.

At six o'clock, it was time for supper – usually some-thing simple, cooked on the gas ring, a boiled egg perhaps or a whole boiled beetroot doused in vinegar. Sometimes, if I was lucky, the muffin man would come round the square, his basket balanced on his head.

Meanwhile, upstairs in the elegant, panelled drawing room, my mother and Sid, in their Chinese cocktail pyjamas, sat sipping White Ladies and listening to the gramophone while waiting for me to come in for my usual goodnight visit. Before I was allowed in, Nanny would give me a quick check to make sure I was clean and, if not, she'd soon remedy matters with a vigorously spat-on corner of her apron. One day when my mother had important visitors, they were startled by an indignant scream: 'No, Nanny! I *won't* have my face washed with spit!' There was terrible embarrassment all round and Nanny was told that in future she must stick to soap and water.

My visit to the drawing room was usually brief, a nervous peck on Sid's cheek, a loving hug with a goodnight kiss for my mother. After that it was straight up to bed to lie listening to the harpist playing the 'Londonderry Air' in the square below, and watch the lamplighter banishing darkness with each touch of his magic wand. Some hours later, Nanny would come to bed, light a candle, put in her curlers, take out her teeth and kneel to pray. After that we slept soundly till we were woken by the clatter of a horse's hoofs and the shrill cry 'Milk-o!' from Joe the milkman, who would leave the bottles on our doorstep and sneak down the basement steps for a cup of tea with Kathleen. In Victorian times, he would have been known as a 'follower'. Those were the days when no self-respecting servant would answer an advertisement unless it contained the words 'followers permitted'. Both Kathleen and Winnie had quite a few between them, including Harry the coalman, totally black from head to foot and too dirty to be entertained in the servants' parlour. Instead, he was given a special chair next to the range, where he could sit with his filthy boots propped up on it.

The long dark stairway leading to the kitchen was only a stone's throw from my nursery, but my mother had made it quite clear to me that it was forbidden territory. This, of course, made it seem even more alluring. One day, remembering how Alice fell down the rabbit hole and landed in Wonderland, I decided to take the plunge. Much to my delight, I was given a wonderfully warm welcome by both staff and followers alike. Comfortably ensconced in the servants' parlour, with its picture of the Virgin Mary and its well-stocked drinks cupboard, I was given small nips of port or British sherry and nibbled on crystallised violets while Winnie entertained me with choice morsels of gossip about my mother's friends.

Kathleen retired to the kitchen to prepare lunch, and soon a strong smell of boiling cabbage filled the basement. She had no time for what she described as 'foreign muck' and stuck to traditional English dishes – roast beef with Yorkshire pudding, shepherd's pie and steak and kidney pudding. Everything came with overboiled vegetables. Salad was practically unknown, and as for garlic, it was a word you sometimes used while telling a rude joke about 'Frog food'. There were only five sauces: apple with pork, horseradish with beef, mint with lamb, bread sauce with chicken and, of course, Heinz ketchup with Friday's fish. Puddings were always served with lashings of Bird's custard, and fruit salad was rarely seen.

After lunch, it was time for my walk with Nanny and Lucky. There were no parks near us so we usually ended up in the cemetery. Here I could feed the squirrels and steal small bits of marble from the graves. These I left on my windowsill, hoping for a ghost to reclaim them. But, of course, they never did.

Finally, when I was seven, Mummy allowed me to stay up for dinner and the wonderful games that followed it. She was immensely creative and had no time for simple things like board games. Instead she built a small puppet theatre, ideal for Punch and Judy, and hung up a brightly lit sheet for shadow plays. She even bought a little cine-camera. Unfortunately, the films we made always seemed to star Granny in some voluptuous role, Cleopatra or the Queen of Sheba, while I had to be content with the part of her humble serving-maid. Meanwhile the gramophone was playing non-stop, until Iris, tired of winding it up and changing the needle, threw herself on to the sofa, seized her ukulele and gave us an impassioned rendering of 'Pale hands I Loved Beside the Shalimar'.

My mother was keen on all living creatures. As well as dogs and cats, we had lizards who ate mealworms from Harrods or garden worms dug up by Brady, tree-frogs with long tongues for catching flies, and silkworms, to which we fed mulberry leaves stolen from Thomas More's garden on the Embankment.

All this was good fun, but growing older had its disadvantages. Both my mother and Sid were still devout Catholics and they seemed to think it was about time I took my religion seriously. They began by teaching me the Catechism, which was not a great success. 'Joan learns quickly and easily,' my mother wrote, 'but unfortunately she refuses to admit that lying and disobedience are sins. We had a big row over this!' Sid, who had recently published a book entitled *Guilt*, was horrified to hear how little I seemed to understand this, and decided it was about time she taught me a few lessons. If I asked for a second helping at dinner, that was Greed. Lying on the sofa was pure Laziness. Too many check-ups in the mirror showed Vanity. But my worst sin, apparently, was Selfishness. Once, when reaching up to pick a rose, I knocked down a caterpillar and accidentally trod on it. Sid, who was watching, looked at me in horror: 'You see, Joan,' she said, 'all you can think of is getting your own way no matter what pain this causes to others.' Even hugging my mother was made to seem a sin. She worried endlessly about my mother's health and sent me a poem that started:

> I must not leap on Mummy
> Like a stupid ten stone ass.
> For Mummy is a brittle thing,
> Six feet of shining glass.

I must not sit at table
And stuff as pigs do stuff,
But only ask for more
If Mummy's had enough.

Fortunately, my mother was far more understanding. 'Joan,' she wrote, 'behaves like a little devil but I notice that her sense of values is altering very much for the better and all her naughtiness is only an effort to hide some good impulse that she is subconsciously ashamed of.'

Then something happened that put me beyond blame: I contracted severe bronchitis and had to stay in bed, looked after by a trained nurse. *I* soon recovered but the effect on my mother was disastrous. With no Dick to worry about, all her anxieties were now centred on me. She told Sid that I had only to cough to make her feel like throwing herself under a car. It came to the point where I didn't dare to clear my throat in her presence. Finally, Sid was so worried that she called in a doctor, who said that if my mother was to preserve her health and sanity, I must be sent away. Sid saw this as her big chance to get rid of me and have Iris to herself. At the age of seven I was sent as a weekly boarder to a nearby convent. My weekends were still spent at home, but every Sunday night a taxi would arrive to take me to the Convent of the Assumption a few streets away. I couldn't understand why I had to leave my cosy home and climb the dark stairway to where a hard-faced nun was waiting for me with a bowl of bread and milk, and a pitcher of ice-cold water for me to wash in.

As taxi-time came near, I developed terrible pains in my stomach, but somehow this was kept from my mother, and Sid used to make a big joke of it – 'Butterflies in your tummy again,' she would say, with a mocking laugh.

In fact, the convent was quite a friendly place but I learnt very little there, as we were taught something called the Montessori method, mainly threading beads on wires or piecing together bits of coloured plastic. Then in the afternoon, it was rounders, played on a gravel pitch so you grazed your knees every time you fell. The nuns would stand by with bottles of iodine and if you screamed with pain you were told to offer up your suffering to Jesus.

Then, when I was nine, the time came for me to make my first communion, and to purify myself in readiness for this great occasion, I had first to go to confession. This posed a few problems. Father Corato was a friend of the family and would certainly recognise my voice in the con-fessional. So anything *too* monstrous was ruled out. I tried my best to think of some sin that wasn't too shocking – Vanity perhaps? Then I remembered an entry in my mother's Baby's Progress Book. 'Joan has very hairy arms and legs, fat tummy, slight squint and a peculiar walk.' Vanity was definitely out.

I knew that I was greedy: as all through Mass I thought of nothing but the wonderful hot breakfast that was to follow and the words '*Ite, missa est*' – 'Go, the Mass is ended' – meant only one thing: Wall's chipolata sausages. But Greed, too, was out: Father Corato came to tea with us every Saturday, and I didn't want his beady eyes on me while I was trying to sneak my third slice of Fuller's walnut cake.

There was, of course, something called Indecent Thoughts, but thoughts about what? Pee-pee and doo-doos came to mind, but surely there must be worse things than that. Finally I settled for three good old standbys, rudeness, disobedience and laziness, and was awarded the statutory penance of three Hail Marys and one Our Father.

So, now I was considered pure enough to make my first holy communion – 'the happiest day of your life,' Sid assured me. I wore a long white dress with a veil to match. The dress was beautiful but, unfortunately, had no pockets so I had to keep my hankie stuffed into my knickers.

After receiving the Holy Eucharist, I was hurrying down the long corridor towards a tempting breakfast when I suddenly got the sniffles. I heaved up my skirts and was feeling around in my knickers when Mother Mary Theresa swept round the corner. Her terrifying voice froze me in my tracks. 'Joan! You filthy child! Take your hand out immediately. Don't you know that you are committing a mortal sin? And with the Holy Child Jesus still inside you!'

During breakfast my mother noticed that I was quiet, thoughtful and very pale. I knew I had committed a sin and should seek forgiveness for it, but how could I when I had no idea what I had done?

Obviously there was something wicked between my legs, but what? One night, determined to find out, I lay on top of the eiderdown, lifted my nightie and explored the forbidden area. Just then, my mother came in to kiss me good night. As she bent over me she froze in horror. 'Take your hand out immediately!' she cried. 'You're playing with yourself, aren't you? Don't you know it's a sin?'

She left the room without kissing me, and suddenly something broke inside me. I had never before said a bad word to my mother but now I found myself kneeling at the end of my bed screaming, 'Beast! Swine! I hate you!'

My mother stopped half-way down the stairs, then ran up again, her long legs taking the stairs two at a time. She dragged me off the bed, threw me across her knee and gave me a good hard spanking. I kept twisting round, trying to see her face. Would it be the face I knew and loved, or would anger have made it unrecognisable? But I could only reach as high as her shoulder. She was wearing her favourite Romanian blouse and although, at that moment, she seemed like a stranger, the red and black pattern was reassuringly familiar.

My mother and I were soon friends again but I was left with the knowledge that I had committed a sin, and as I had no idea how to confess it, I would end up burning in Purgatory.

I had always been terrified of fire, ever since I heard about the Crystal Palace being burnt down. I visualised Purgatory as a long room, the length of a school hall, with a cement floor dotted with little holes. Underneath the floor a fire was raging and the heads of the sinners protruded through the holes like so many well-smoked kippers.

Every night, I knelt at the end of my bed, praying desperately that I might be spared Purgatory. Then one night a tall dark man appeared in my dreams, telling me that if I wished to be forgiven I must punish myself now, in this life. I tried hard to hurt myself, but what could I do with only a blue silk dressing-gown cord at my disposal? Eventually, in despair, I used to climb on to the bedhead and, after a quick prayer for forgiveness, hurl myself off to drown in the swirling eiderdown sea below.

Slowly, my guilt subsided and the tall dark man shrank until he was the size of a cockroach and quietly scuttled away. After that I became a normal happy child again with only one aberration: a morbid obsession with punishment.

I tried hard to keep this a secret but one day, while we were staying in the country with Uncle Basil, my godfather, I blew my cover. He had a magnificent library and as a farewell gesture he told me I could choose any book from it that I wanted. My mother smiled – *The Lives of the Saints*, perhaps, or some charming book about flowers and animals? She was chatting to some highly respectable friends when I proudly emerged bearing a huge, vividly illustrated tome of Chinese tortures. My mother was appalled. 'Take it back immediately,' she cried, 'and change it for something more suitable.' I finally opted for *Gulliver's Travels* – after all, it was a classic so it must be all right.

Unfortunately, soon after I got it home, my mother opened it, and discovered a picture of a tiny Lilliputian Gulliver climbing the naked body of a Brobdingnagian beauty and looking with admiration and amazement at her enormous nipples. So that, too, was confiscated and it was back to *Peter Pan* and *Alice*.

Soon after my tenth birthday, I was given some alarming news. My days at The Assumption were over and instead I was to go to what they described as a proper boarding-school, the Convent of the Holy Child Jesus in St Leonards-on-Sea, where the nuns were known as female Jesuits. I found them friendly, humorous and broad-minded – it was my fellow schoolmates who made my life a torment, teasing and bullying me without mercy. Unfortunately I can't blame them, when I remember how I looked – long greasy plaits, goggles and a brace on my front teeth. I also had a funny way of walking, with my head bent to one side. But worst of all – unforgivable – I was brainy and a swot. In fact, I was the most unpopular girl in the school, apart from Betty Rees-Mogg, known as the Greasy Wog. This may sound harsh, but in those days we usually called foreigners wogs or dagos. Much of my spare time was spent crying in the loos or 'blubbing in the Jeyes', as we used to call it.

Then, one day, salvation arrived. Lots of the girls belonged to secret societies, but one group stood out from the others, the exotic and much admired Bitchum Whorums, or BWs, as they were called. To my utter joy and amazement, they spotted me as a kindred spirit and I was invited to join their ranks. After that there was no more teasing – I had become a sort of protected species for no one messed with the BWs. They had all adopted glamorous names: Nefertiti, Jezebel or Titsy-Tahiti, but I, being Wynd-ham, had to be content with Breeze-Bacon.

We also had our own language. Anything delicious was 'squeegee'. Pious ladies were Church Cats, and the holy pictures we loved were, rather curiously, known as Jellies. As in 'Darling Jezebel. Thanks for the squeegee Jellies.' Our main activities consisted of smoking furiously behind the games pavilion or combing the library for books with juicy bits in them.

It turned out to be a pretty fruitless search. There was good old Onan 'casting his seed on to the ground'. We imagined this to be a bit like the stuff you fed canaries with, which didn't quite fit in with our current theory of how the dreaded act was performed, involving a complicated contraption of bubbling phials and tubes. Considering our pet tortoises in the garden were at it all the time, I can only be amazed at our *naïveté*. There was also a rather boring brothel scene in Shakespeare's *Measure for Measure*, but best of all, or so we had hoped, was Dante's *Inferno* illustrated by Gustav Doré, with hundreds of naked bodies writhing in torment. Unfortunately some lucky nun had been given the task of scratching out every single you-know-what with a pin. What a lovely time she must have had!

But things got better during the hols, and the big breakthrough came one night at bath-time when I discovered Freud's *Interpretation of Dreams* in Sid's study next to the bathroom. I'd already run my bath so I sat on the edge splashing merrily away with one hand and turning the pages with the other. Weird words like 'masturbation' and 'orgasm' swam before my eyes. I also became aware that the whole house must be seething with erotic objects. Everything over six inches long, from a cucumber to a corkscrew, was a symbol of you-know-what. I knew exactly what a you-know-what looked like, as I had seen Greek statues, but I had no idea what it was for. And as for snakes and stallions, I realised with a stab of guilt that every single dream I had ever had had been a potential mortal sin. There was also a piece about candles and what girls did with them – so it wasn't canary seed or test-tubes, it had been candles all the time! I couldn't wait to tell the Bitchum Whorums. Sid had other books by Freud, which I leafed through in the privacy of the bathroom, but they were not at all juicy, rather boring in fact, so finally I gave up and went back to washing. Much, I imagine, to everyone's relief.

Back at school, my first thought was to get hold of the BWs to tell them the news. They thought it all very funny and interesting, but it was only about Sex, not Love, and all of us were madly, though innocently, in love with older girls. This was called being cracked on someone, and my crack was the charismatic sixth-former Rosemary Dwyer. She, of course, was unaware of my feelings. In fact, we had hardly ever spoken to each other and I thought myself lucky if I could steal a blonde hair off the back of her tunic, to be kept hidden in my desk like some holy relic. Laundry day was also full of possibilities: if I was clever enough to spot Rosemary's clean underpants, I could thrust my hand in and not wash it for a week.

But the highlight was Friday night in the dorm, when it was Rosemary's turn to make the sign of the cross on our foreheads and kiss us good night. The first time I was caught napping, with greasy hair, grubby nightdress, crumpled sweet wrappers and the *Girls' Own* comic on my bedside table, but by the following Friday I was ready for her: freshly washed hair spread out on the pillow, a spotless nightie patterned with roses, and Jane Austen beside me on the table.

Luckily the nuns had nothing against us being cracked. They probably knew how innocent our feelings were. Mother Damien, the headmistress, was particularly broad-minded and understanding, and we looked forward to what she called her 'little chats'.

Usually she lost no time in getting to the point. 'I suppose Rosemary still fills your mind, morning, noon and night?'

'Yes,' I said.

'But what is it you like about her?'

'Everything,' I replied. 'I would gladly sit on spikes for her sake!'

'Well,' said Mother Damien, 'if you want *my* opinion, I think she would get much more benefit if you didn't talk at Study, for instance, than if you sat on spikes. Because sitting on spikes and hurting yourself is probably your natural inclination. You're getting a terrible delight from doing things to prove your love by the bond of blood. Why don't you do something normal and sensible for her instead?'

I tried hard to be sensible about Rosemary, but the obsession continued. I even lost interest in the BWs:

Titsy Tahiti (real name Thetis!) doesn't see much of them either. I always thought that she was much too 'naice' and lady-like to be a Bitchum Whorum. She and her family actually <u>dress</u> for dinner <u>every</u> night! She never goes to a film unless it is in German or Yiddish or something equally incomprehensible, which means it is so good and consequently so dull it has been awarded a gold medal. As a result, they've elected two new members – Annie McSqueegee and Katy Fitzwhorum.

But I had gone one better: I had acquired, for the very first time in my life, a Best Friend. Surprisingly enough, it was Anne Dawson who, at one time, had been my chief tormentor. 'I used to loathe you like fire and brimstone. I thought you were poisonous,' she told me, 'but now I'd like us to be chums!' It started by just saying good night or going to church together but now we went on long walks round the garden, feeding our tortoises and talking about our cracks.

Anne: 'Do you think *Love* is like this, Joan?'

Me (with conviction): '*Yes*, I certainly do!'

What with Rosemary and Anne, and everybody being 'absolutely spiffing' to me, it was a really happy term. The only cloud on the horizon was my music teacher, Mother Aloysius – known as Shar: she had hated me right from the start because I was brilliant at sight-reading, which she looked upon as a form of cheating. To her satisfaction, I was appallingly bad at scales, and she would stand over me with a ruler hitting my knuckles every time I struck a wrong note.

There was a picture of Beethoven over the piano, glaring down at me like an infuriated ape with gleaming malevolent eyes. I used to glare back at him. 'All right,' I'd say. 'I know you hate me – well, I hate you too, like stink. And what's more I enjoy playing my scales badly, just to make you and all those other highbrow musical geniuses squirm in their frames. Grrrr! Bah! Pish!' This gave me infinite satisfaction.

Because of my good sight-reading, I was chosen to play the piano in the school orchestra. I enjoyed it enormously, but after a couple of terms Shar decided to replace me. 'But don't worry, Joan,' she said, 'we wouldn't like you to be left out altogether. How about the triangle?' I knew exactly what that meant: you were perched right up at the top in full view of everyone, with about two pings per concert and all your friends in the front row laughing and jeering. As a result of this humiliation, I lost interest in the classical music I had loved. Instead of Mozart and Beethoven, I now found myself twiddling away at the wireless in search of nigger jazz, as we called it, meaning pop music given a shot in the arm by new black talented musicians like Ray Charles, Louis Armstrong and Charlie Parker.

It was the summer term of 1934. 'There's nothing to say <u>at all</u>,' I wrote to my mother. 'It's too hot and nothing ever happens. I just slink around, looking very untidy, exchange bawdy pleasantries with my friends, eat enormously, work occasionally, and annoy Shar continuously. In fact it's all rather boring.'

Then something exciting did happen. I woke up one morning to find my sheets soaked in blood. I was terrified, thinking I'd burst an artery. Then the penny dropped – I'd got the curse! I wrapped a towel between my legs and raced down to the San where Matron gave me a packet of STs (sanitary towels) and told me to have a good wash.

An hour later I was summoned to Reverend Mother's study. I stood in front of her desk, shifting nervously from foot to foot and wondering what the hell I'd done now. Reverend Mother Celine – the Sea Lion – looked up and fixed me with a steely glare. 'Matron has been to see me,' she said, 'and she tells me you have blasphemed. Apparently you told her that you had got "the curse"!'

'What *should* I call it?'

'You will call it your "monthly period". Now, to atone for your blasphemy you will stand for half an hour in front of the altar and say the five Sorrowful Mysteries of the Rosary. May God forgive you for your sin!'

I stood in the aisle fumbling with my beads, and tried to remember what my mother had called it. Oh, yes. It had been 'Alex' or, more often, 'dear old Alex', a name she had seen on her very first packet of STs. I didn't stay for the full half-hour as I was hungry and the chapel was cold. I couldn't wait to rush down, find my friends, especially the BWs, and shout to them the exciting news: 'I've got the curse!'

When my mother heard about it, she decided it was time I was taught the facts of life. So, during the next holidays, she drove me round and round Hyde Park in her little Austin Seven, furiously revving the engine to hide her embarrassment.

Apparently it was not birdseed, test-tubes *or* candles. It was you-know-what: the man put it you-know-where and implanted his seed. 'But,' she went on, 'you mustn't worry. It's quite natural. Just like animals.' This seemed to be her favourite phrase as she said it several times. However, she continued, I must be careful. She warned me to be particularly careful with men in taxis: 'But you know when they're going to pounce – they give off this funny sort of smell!' She signed off with a final reassurance that it was 'just like animals, darling', and took me home for a nice cup of tea. I was now seeing my pets in a totally new light. Perhaps I should get Punky, my rabbit, a wife?

It was during the following Easter term that I noticed some rather worrying changes in Rosemary Dwyer's behaviour. She was no longer laughing and joking with her friends. She was not taking part in any of the school plays – in fact, she seemed to spend most of her time kneeling alone in the chapel. Apparently she had a 'vocation' and in a few months' time she would take the veil. When advised that she was too young for such a step, she insisted that she wanted to give her youth to God.

On the morning of her Clothing Ceremony, we inundated her with bunches of spring flowers and lovingly inscribed Jellies. Later, watching from the gallery, we saw her first as a Bride of Christ, dressed all in white with a flowing veil crowned with a wreath of lilies. But all too soon she had to make tracks for the sacristy where Mother Damien was waiting for her with a pair of sharp scissors to cut off her lovely blonde hair. An almost unrecognisable figure emerged, dressed in black, which prostrated itself in front of the altar under a flower-strewn pall surrounded by a group of nuns singing the 'De Profundis' to signify that Rosemary – no, sorry, Sister Mary Josephine – was now dead to the world.

I went into breakfast in floods of tears but was soon surrounded by a swarm of BWs laughing and dancing round me. 'No more bad behaviour now. She's married to the Saviour now!' they sang. Still in tears, I couldn't eat a thing. Some kind friend had smuggled me in a slice of Rosemary's 'wedding cake' but it would have seemed sacrilege to eat it, so I wrapped it in a paper napkin to keep as a memento of one of the saddest days of my life.

I tried hard to become my normal happy self again, but one thing was still worrying me:

Darling Mummy, do you think you recognise people who you knew on Earth and like them just as much in Heaven? Or does one only think of God and nothing else? I pray like mustard for her all during Mass and Benediction, and any Indulgences and Graces that I get I offer up for her. You see, I'll never speak to her again on Earth, so when I get to Heaven, I'm hoping that she'll recognise me, and thank me for getting her a higher place there. Then I'll run into her arms and <u>she</u>'ll be part of the Beatific Vision. That's my one and only hope. But I'll have to die first.

Darling [my mother wrote back in some alarm],
Please try to curb your desire to die! As you must realise
you are still very precious to <u>me</u>! I certainly don't want to
die yet. I feel there is so much I still want to do and see
before I fold my hands in peace. There are also a few
people I should hate to leave, and last but not least I hope
to last out to see the day when you present me with
grandchildren, which I shall probably spoil most horribly
much to your disgust!! You ask me about Heaven – of
course no-one really knows, but I can't imagine we'll just
be sitting on clouds thinking about God. I'm sure you'll
be re-united with everyone you loved in life – Rosemary
included.

This letter cheered me enormously – though I wasn't
too keen on the grandchildren idea. By now, Iris was writing me the most wonderful letters two or three times a
week. If Sid had thought that by sending me away she
would create a rift between us, she had another think
coming. On the contrary. While we lived together, we had
always found it difficult to discuss our intimate thoughts
and feelings, but letters were different: without any embarrassing eye-contact you could let all your most secret hopes
and fears flood out on to the paper. At first I addressed her
formally as 'Dear Mother' but soon it became 'Darling
Mother', 'My own Darling Mummy', and finally, 'Darling,

Delicious, Scrummy Old Mummy! Thank God we are more like sisters and can say what we like to one another. Goodbye, you funny old darling devil!'

Iris loved animals as much as I did, and took great care of my various pets while I was away. Every now and then, I would get a running report on their welfare and habits:

The mice are still without children. I think that maybe they are both gentlemen, so we can't expect too much! But they play, and make and remake their nests and smell pretty high! One of them seems to be getting a bit mangy and losing his fur — he also scratches a lot. Do you think he needs a tonic? Punky is very well and has a lovely trick of holding one ear down with his paw while he cleans it. The cat never leaves his side. Don't worry about your fish. I bought them a packet of dead flies, which smell awful but they seem to love them and come rushing to the surface with goggling eyes whenever they see me coming.

She also loved keeping me up to date with what she called her 'Garden News':

One marrow seed in my little wooden box has shown a green blade! Great excitement. Am now waiting for the milkman's horse to give necessary manure for further

*progress of same! There are yellow patches on the lawn
caused, I fear, by the dogs. Otherwise grass is lush and
green. Punky now sits up and begs for dandelion leaves.
Varnished garden seat – and sat on it too soon! Ruined
my best skirt! Also destroyed by accident spider's nest on
seat, about a thousand baby spiders with varnish on their
legs. Very sad. Put them out of their misery. Mrs
Beswick from next door came for a glass of sherry in the
garden. Got so happy and hilarious that while she was
leaning over to look at my nurstursians (spelling?) she
made a misplaced confidence! Do you understand my
cryptic wording? Very embarrassing. Enjoyed hosing the
nasty ginger cat off the wall – crept up on him, and let
fly!*

Even her letters on serious topics often ended on a
lighter note:

*The next two or three years will be awfully important, as
the 'real you' will finally emerge. I am so hoping and
praying that it will be the 'you' that is the best one. I
find wherever one goes, one is always coming across dirty-
minded people, bad influences and all sorts of filth in
fact. But it won't affect your character really, provided
you keep your soul polished up – then the dirt won't
stick!*

*Now, I must tell you that the privet moth cocoon is still
alive and wiggling its tail! I am so <u>thrilled</u> as he ought to
be out any minute now.*

My own letters, I regret to say, were always full of
urgent demands. Money, of course, was always welcome,
and so were sweets, particularly in Lent when the tuck
cupboard was locked. I also craved Marmite and something called Radio Malt. 'Yo-yos,' I wrote, 'are now back in
fashion. I desperately need new strings.' I also begged her to
keep her eyes skinned for deodorants, especially the Odo-
Ro-No brand, Kirbigrips and eyebrow tweezers. 'A
tortoiseshell slide from Woolworths would be spiffing, but
most of all, I'd love you to send me some slimming cream.'
I'd recently taken a good look at my figure in the glass and
was a little bit worried about the size of my bottom.

Iris not only found the cream, but disguised it in a box
of cough lozenges in case the nuns should spot it and cause
me embarrassment. 'Do you only use it on your backside?'
she asked anxiously. 'You won't over-do it, will you?'

Most of my thank-you letters to her were suitably
enthusiastic: 'Darling Mummy, You are a pearl among
mothers. When I opened your letter and that ten shilling
note fell out, I practically swooned with joy!' Others were
less ecstatic. 'Thank you frightfully for your letters and the
soap. I was *so* disappointed when I opened the parcel and it

was only soap! Will you send me some fudge soon from that little shop where you got it last time?'

I tried not to ask for money too often as I knew Mummy was not very well off. Much of her capital had been rashly invested in Romanian Railways, and Dick, of course, was always late with his maintenance payments. I also had a strong suspicion that she was keeping Sid. Sometimes I was sorely tempted – as when half the school went on a pilgrimage to Rome. But thirteen pounds and elevenpence? I didn't bother to mention it to her!

My teeth were a bit of a worry too. 'I do hope,' she wrote, 'that your new plate isn't going to cost too much or I shan't be able to afford my new car. Poor old Noah is practically falling to pieces. And Granny has already bought herself a new white flying helmet in anticipation. What shall we call the next one – did Noah have a wife?'

A new car was not her only extravagance. 'I am buying a beautiful new wireless on the instalment system. It is clear as a bell and jets all round Europe. It only arrived tonight and when I have finished this letter, I'm going on a journey round the Continent!' Of course she could have sold some of her jewellery – she had ropes of real pearls and the beautiful diamond brooch given to her by the Prince of Wales – but she preferred to keep them for the very few grand occasions that came her way.

Darling,
The other night I went to a film premiere with Granny.
'Three Smart Girls'. It <u>was</u> all very smart. Everyone stared
around at everybody else and was dressed to the nines in
sables and jewels. Granny looked like a duchess in furs and
brocade and had her photo flashed by a newshound. I also
dressed myself up and even had a train! Diamonds flashed
in my hair and on my bosom! The film was nothing to rave
about except for the voice of a new young actress of fourteen
called Deanna Durbin who sang like a bird.

Although I was still quite enjoying school, I found myself longing desperately for the hols – especially Christmas! Every morning I would tick off the days on my calendar. Three more weeks, sixteen more days, three more days and then, at last, 'The smell of a dusty train. London bridge over the cold silver river, my darling Thames, with the scent of cocoa and coffee from the great warehouses on the banks rushing in on an icy wind through the open window. Grime and hum and roar and Charing Cross and Mummy and Home!'

The Fulham Road was the same as ever with all the old familiar faces: the French boy with the black beret and the strings of onions, the toffee-apple man, the postman who barked like a dog, and the hordes of dirty little boys who were always sponging on Kathleen for cake and selling us firewood.

At home the main change was that my nanny was now my mother's lady's maid, and ironed her nightie while she was taking her nightly bath, and my granny had installed an amazing electric slimming machine with wide rubber bands that strapped her in and massaged her hips. I can't say I noticed much difference.

25 December This morning I woke to see a white glare through a crack in the blinds. With a whoop of joy, I flung open the window to find the whole world covered in snow — real Christmas weather! I took up great handfuls of it from the sill and buried my face in its coolness like Garbo in Queen Christina. The pillowcase at the end of my bed was bulging with parcels. There was a lovely smell of frying sausages and all the animals were wearing little red satin bows round their necks. Lunch was delicious. Roast turkey and a home-made Christmas pudding so full of little silver lucky charms — sixpenny pieces, wedding rings or thimbles — that you almost cracked your teeth on it. Afterwards, we clipped the wax candles onto the Christmas tree, making sure that they were straight so as not to drop wax on the carpet. Underneath was a crib with wooden figures carved

by Sid and piles and piles of presents. We had all
made long lists of what we wanted, and I had asked
Mummy to warn Jessie *not* to give me her usual girls'
books, the *Schoolgirls' Own*, or the *Big Book for Girls*. I
had also asked, rather optimistically, for a black halo
hat, a gold signet ring and Baudelaire's *Fleurs du Mal*.
I didn't get the ring but I got the other two. (I
wonder why I like Baudelaire so much. Why is evil
so attractive to me? I mustn't succumb or I shall be
damned! Please, God, keep me always safe from its
corruption.) I also got some nice chocs and a holy
card from two of the Bitchum Whorums. 'Darling
Breeze-Bacon. This Christmas Jelly is in memory of
all the squeegee times we had last term – smoking in
Savernake forest and plucking our eyebrows. Have a
ripping Christmas with lots of love from Titsy and
Jezebel.'

Later on, lots of Mummy's friends came round
for cocktails. They were a rather strange crew as
usual – Alfred and his friend Bertie, who wasted no
time in rushing upstairs and trying on Mummy's
evening dresses, Polly, who has an Eton crop and
breeds bull terriers, and Isla from Anglesey who has
to shave twice a day. After dinner – cold turkey and
mince pies – we gave our usual Christmas concert
and everybody had to sing a favourite song. Sid's was

'Please Mr Burglar, Don't Steal My Prayer Book!'
and I did my version of 'After the Ball' to wild
applause.

> After the ball is over.
> See her take out her glass eye
> Put her false teeth in the water.
> Cork up the bottle of dye.
> Prop her false leg in the corner
> Hang up her hair on the wall.
> Then all that is left goes to bye-byes
> After the Ball.

Mummy sang 'Indian Love Lyrics' to her ukulele,
and Henry brought the house down with his ever
popular rendering of 'There are Fairies at the Bottom
of my Garden'. Soon after we all went up to bed to
drink Eno's and lie listening to the carol singers in the
street below. It has been a wonderful Christmas!

Of course there were some presents that we didn't like
but had to be polite about: 'Dear Aunt Flossie, Thanks
awfully for the tartan sewing bag and the dear little bear
with pins for whiskers. It was just what I wanted.'

As soon as it was over, we made our plans for New
Year's Eve. We usually started the evening at a Russian

restaurant because, as my mother would say, 'I love music that gets really worked up, interspersed with wild cries and yells of excitement. All that eternal Jazz with "Yew" and "Blew" gets a bit boring! So I'll book a table at the Troika and we'll all sweep in in our velvet dresses!'

New Year's Eve Granny, determined that I should look my best, sent me to her beauty specialist who attacked my face with a pair of tweezers, plucking out my eyebrows and putting black muck on my lashes! After a wonderful meal – caviar, vodka and gypsy music – we made our way to Piccadilly Circus, to see the New Year in.

1 January After we had recovered from our hangovers, we set to work on our New Year Resolutions. Sid's was to give up smoking! Some hope, as she's up to fifty a day. Mummy found it difficult because she never seems to do anything wrong anyway. Mine on the other hand was easy – Shar had constantly accused me of being coarse, vulgar and a bad example to other girls so these were my resolutions. 'I must give up those orgies of plain speaking in the library, letting the whole world know that my father was an adulterer, revelling in his reflected evil. I must also stop discussing the facts of life with the BWs. The strange thing is that inside I'm really quite pure but even outwardly I must try to be so.

During the Easter term, there was no one on the scene to be cracked on so I decided I might as well live up to my New Year resolutions. I avoided the BWs and mixed instead with a rather boring group of girls, who took their religion very seriously. I even started saying morning and evening prayers, something I hadn't done for a long time but I remembered how they used to go: 'Darling Jesus. I never feel very nice in the mornings, but I know that You will make me happy and I offer the whole of my day to You, whence it came. Please make everyone very nice to me today and please don't let me get into any rows with Shar or Sea Lion. I love You with all my heart and I'm very sorry if I have ever hurt You. Amen.' Then, in the evening, 'Darling Jesus, my Lord and Master. I'm comfortably in bed and very happy. Today was lovely and I thank You for it with all my heart for I know that all my happiness comes from You. Please, dear Jesus, make my future happy too.'

In the past, I'd always been a religious child. The Bible stories seemed to me something out of fairyland: the baby in his cot, watched over by his two pet animals, with fairies called angels fluttering overhead. And the three kings bringing those disappointing Christmas presents. What on earth was 'murr'? As he grew older, I tried to imagine what he looked like – and usually ended up with a boy who resembled Peter Pan, but with longer hair and wearing a nightdress. Later, when he grew a beard, he became a famous magician. I thought his tricks were marvellous, especially when he got dead men to jump out of their graves, but I wasn't so keen on the loaves and fishes . . . just bread and fish? No butter, no tomato ketchup? Definitely *not* one of his better performances.

The crucifixion was never mentioned. That came much later – when the nuns realised how useful it would be if we thought of pain as a good thing. This came in handy if we were ill, or on visits to the dentist who yanked out our teeth without any painkillers. We screamed and sobbed in agony, but the nun sitting in the corner went on rattling her beads and told us to offer up our pain to Jesus who had died for us on the cross.

But now it was spring, and I could sit in the garden with my new friends. The sun was shining and the daffodils and bluebells were all coming into bloom. We said our rosaries and wrote in our 'retreat books' and had a 'spiffing' time. There were also processions for the Feast of Our Lady. I wrote in my book:

As we walked round the garden in procession, past the crisp pale green leaf-buds and flaming crocuses, singing the Lourdes hymn, I suddenly felt that I was taking part in some old Pagan ritual in honour of the Earth's regeneration. I realised that men had always worshipped the same gods, though under different names. 'Ave Maria' or 'Io Pan!', the impulse is still the same whether we celebrate Spring's return among the convent crocuses or the Grecian Asphodel.

I reread this entry a few weeks later, took a large black crayon and wrote in capital letters in the margin: 'OH MY GOD. WHAT UTTER BILGE!' Obviously my pious phase had come to a sudden end and I was soon back behaving badly with the BWs.

Edie, Hilary, Thetis and me are great friends now – we are really rather Angela Brazil the way we write to each other in code and discuss Men – rather ridiculous but I suppose we're just the age for it. I've been asked so many times by Edie who <u>mine</u> is. Finally, I was so embarrassed that I had to invent one. I suppose it is rather silly to kiss each other good morning and goodnight the way we do. We are all very different really. Edie is the essence of frivolity, adores men and going to dances. She has French blood and likes men

with beards and pork pie hats. Hilary is half and half.
She likes balloon dancing and Jazz but can talk equally
well about modern art. Thetis, of course, is an out and
out highbrow, <u>very</u> superior. <u>I</u> am anything I like to
be – can enjoy and adjust myself to anybody and
anything, thank God!

Best news of all, I've got a new crack! She's called Jane
Drummond and used to be RD's best friend.
Unfortunately, I think she, too, has a vocation so I won't
have her for very long. Still, it's better than nothing!

It had all started at dancing class when she held my hand
in the Paul Jones and I felt that good old crackation thrill
running through me. I thought I'd managed to keep it a
secret, until Mummy showed me a letter she'd had from
Mother Damien. At first I thought it was just her usual end-
of-term report on my progress in class, and very flattering it
was too: 'She has been working quite well this term and I'm
hoping she will come out top of her class. She certainly has
the best brains in her form. In fact I think she has one of the
most original and interesting minds I have come across.'
Then came the crunch: 'Unfortunately her romantic ten-
dencies are inclined to take her mind off the drudgery of the
classroom! I rather gather that Jane Drummond has super-
seded Rosemary Dwyer in her affections but I do not think
she knows that I have observed this!'

JOAN WYNDHAM

As soon as I could get Damien alone, I taxed her with it. 'How did you know?' I asked her. 'Are you a Sorceress?' She told me that she had known about Jane ever since she saw me dancing with her. The way I did it! Immediately she knew! It's hardly safe to <u>think</u> with a woman like that around! Towards the end of our talk she got frightfully affectionate and put her arm on my shoulder and fiddled with my hair and as we went out together she took my hand and gave it an awfully big squeeze. She said lots more which I can't possibly put down, but which made me feel awfully nice inside.

Several weeks later, I had something new to report: 'It's all very well being cracked on other girls, but now, at last, I'm in love with a Real Live Man!! He is a young English actor called John Gielgud whom I have seen once before in *Richard of Bordeaux*.'

When I saw that he was doing *Hamlet* at the New I remembered him as being pretty smashing and begged Mummy to get us a couple of seats. I had never seen *Hamlet* before, so I spent several days poring over an old annotated edition, which told you what all the strange words and phrases meant. As a special treat, my mother lashed out and bought stalls seats so we had a wonderful view, and even with an enormous down-curving staircase dominating half

106

the stage, I could still make out a little figure in black, sitting reading in the darkness below it. Then, after a crash of drums and a blare of trumpets, the whole court, headed by the king and queen, swept down the staircase in a riot of colour to the sound of Handel's 'Water Music'. All was going well until Hamlet rose, and stalked across the stage towards his mother's throne. Oh dear! Those legs! Those knees! Had no kind friend warned him against wearing tights on stage? But soon he began his soliloquy, and after that nothing seemed to matter but the beauty of his voice, and by the time it died away on 'the rest is silence', I was an ardent fan. As soon as we got home we composed a letter.

Dear John Gielgud,

I hope you don't mind my writing to you, but I just wanted to say how much we enjoyed your performance tonight. It was absolutely brilliant. I would, of course, love a signed photo of you but if you could just write a few words as well? I can't tell you how much it would mean to me! With all my thanks for a memorable evening,

Joan Wyndham, 28 Evelyn Gardens, London SW10

All I got was a signed photo on which I rather successfully forged 'To Joan', copying the letters J, O and N from his signature. I imagined he had some fierce old secretary who kept all trivia from him. Deprived of an answer, I hung around the stage door and when I discovered that he lived quite near, in St Martin's Lane, I sometimes followed him home so that I could kiss his doorknob. I also dragged my unfortunate mother back to see the play again, and of course we had to sit in the front stalls – 'within spitting distance', as I called it. I felt then as if I could go on seeing *Hamlet*, never tire of it and always be thrilled by it, even without John Gielgud. I could even picture myself when I was old, sitting in the gods, munching liver-sausage sandwiches out of a paper bag and gnawing my knuckles with excitement.

It was the summer term when I wrote:

A miracle has happened. Anne, who is also cracked on him, has an aunt with a friend in the cast, and she has promised to take us both backstage to John's dressing room!

The day came, and we asked for John at the stage door and were shown up to his dressing room. He was wearing suede shoes and flannels with a blue dressing gown on top. His figure is marvellous! He still had a bit of makeup on and a sticky forehead where his wig had been.

When he called Anne Miss Dawson, she had the nerve to say, 'Please call me Anne,' but I didn't – I was too shy for such a bold suggestion. However, I did tell him about the dream I'd had last night. I told him I'd been tracking him down and discovered him going into Selfridges to have a Turkish bath, wearing a green and white boater with a feather in it. He thought that was very funny and laughed a lot.

Every now and then he'd look nervously at Gladys (the lady who'd got us in). 'My dear Gladys! Were my legs any better tonight?'

Gladys: 'Oh yes, John. Not bad at all.'

'Thank goodness. You can't <u>imagine</u> what torment the letters I get about my knees give me. I try *so* hard to stand with my knees straight but it's so much easier to have them bent!'

'You see,' Gladys muttered in my ear, 'John is almost but not quite knock-kneed!'

After that it was mainly small-talk about putting central heating into his cottage in Essex, making a film with him playing Christ, or how he moves his court ladies around all the time to stop them getting bored. <u>Bored?</u> They must be mad!

As we left, we looked back and caught him gargling with a whole flagon of port. He saw us watching him, and gave a guilty smile. 'Good for my throat, you know!' he said, and took another large glug.

Anne came back and spent the night with me. We lay in bed and had hysterics. Warm, vibrating, tickling,

paralysing thrills and spasms ran through us – and
what stories we made up!

Inevitably, as a result of this meeting, I became hope-
lessly stagestruck and finally plucked up enough courage to
tell my mother:

*You ask me what I want to do once I leave school? Well,
what I've had in mind for ages, but didn't want to tell you
about it, in case you thought me a fool, is that I want and
<u>mean</u> to go on the stage! I wouldn't even mind very small
parts and I'd work d—n hard to become really good! I don't
worry about school any more. It just doesn't interest me. All
I can think of is the stage and I'm constantly thinking of*
Hamlet. *I need only go into a corner with Shakespeare to
see it all over again, every note of music, every movement,
expression and inflection. It is extraordinary how, once you're
really cracked on a thing, it takes all relish from the other
arts. Since I felt like this, I've completely gone off music, I'm
rather bored with art, never write a line and think it almost
heresy to be enthusiastic over anything else. It's like in* The
Hound of Heaven, *it is 'a weed albeit an amaranthine
weed, suffering no flowers but its own to grow'. It is such a
lovely feeling not caring about anything!*

*When I think of all the marvellous countries that I used
to want to visit, all those sunny, temply, flowery places like*

*Athens, I realise that I'd <u>much rather</u> be sitting on the floor
of a dark theatre, all brown and foggy and lit by gas-lamps
and smelling that wonderful theatre smell than any of
those marvellous places.*

My mother certainly didn't think me a fool, but she
had plenty of good advice for me:

*Don't let John and the stage loom too large in your mind,
blotting out all the other lovely things around you. After
all, Shakespeare could never have written his plays if he
had not been interested in <u>everything</u>! You'll find, I'm
sure, if you open your eyes wide to all the different
interests around you that they will help to fit you for acting
far more than sitting in a corner obsessing yourself with
daydreams.*

I thanked Mummy for her 'learned treatise' but has-
tened to set her right on one or two points:

*No, I don't just sit around daydreaming. It's just that I
feel so happy now, having something to live for, that I can't
be bothered with things that don't really interest me. I
realise that this place isn't the whole world, so why feel
anxious or miserable over silly things like my position in
class? I work just as hard but without caring two d—ns*

whether I fail or pass. I don't dread my music lessons any
more either. I just get what I want from music now and
there's a lot of it that I adore without bothering about
scales or Beethoven. As for studying human nature, I get
quite enough of that from rushing around with my lewd
girlfriends!

My mother seemed delighted to think that I now had
something to live for and look forward to: she had always
prayed that I might have a purposeful life and not fritter it
away like so many other people. 'What fun you must have
planning and wondering about the future,' she wrote. 'I
only hope and pray that it will always be happy for you and
that you will never be disappointed or hurt. But of course
that is too much to hope for, if we never suffered, we would
never realise joys.'

Our end-of-term play was *She Stoops to Conquer* and, to
my immense excitement, I was given the lead part. 'We
have started rehearsals and it is <u>squeegee!</u> I love my part. It
just floats along naturally like a bird. I wish we were doing
it with professionals instead of silly little schoolgirls. The
nicest time for rehearsing is in one's bath.'

Although my mother was delighted to hear how much
I was enjoying my acting, she was also wise enough to
know that I would need an awful lot of serious training if
I was ever to succeed on the stage. She had heard of a

training school called RADA and went there to take a look at it. 'There were two charming common girls in reception, who took me on a guided tour.' (In those days it was perfectly all right to say 'common', not to be rude but as a statement of fact.)

The school seemed quite perfect, so she wrote to tell me all about it, and I was over the moon. 'As you know,' I replied, 'I'd always longed to act, but the thought of actually going on stage seemed too big and out of reach. But now you have mentioned RADA, everything has crystallised. The idea has come down like an angel of salvation – the bridge across the gulf that I've always been waiting for. And if I ever were to get into the same play as Him . . . Well!'

Our summer holidays were always spent at Orchard Close in Wiltshire, the new home of my much-loved grandfather, Colonel Guy 'Woffleboots' Wyndham. 'Boots' referred to a range he had once designed for his soldiers, and 'woffle' came from his special way of talking, which sometimes made it impossible to understand a word he said. He loved to sit in his own special chair beside the fireplace, woffling quietly away while doing *The Times* crossword and dreaming of his next trip to London to see his two great loves, Wagner and the Crazy Gang. My

grandmother, Minnie, had died young and, rather to everyone's surprise, Guy had married Violet Leverson, a lady
fifteen years younger than himself, the daughter of the
Sphinx, the only great female love of Oscar Wilde's life. She
was small and plump with dyed auburn hair, immensely
smart and dedicated to social life, and was known to the
family as Aunt Nose, for reasons obvious to anyone who had
met her.

Every weekend she invited down a host of smart, witty
young men: Collie Knox, the well-known wireless critic;
Robert Byron, 'very precious and annoying'; Teddy
Underdown, the actor, very nice indeed; and, best of all,
the tall, blond and gorgeous Peter Coates. Needless to
say, I became immensely cracked on him but I was a bit
puzzled as to why all his friends referred to him as
'Petticoats'. They were all bronzed and very clever, full of
sophisticated and witty observations – the cream of London
Society in fact – and, consequently, rather tiring to unconventional people like me. But I was soon accepted as a
kindred spirit, once they discovered how good I was at
joining in their clever word games.

However, I really much preferred the company of Guy
and Violet's two young sons, Francis and Hugh, and spent
most of my time having fun with them. I also made friends
with the only girl who was there on her own, Oriel Ross
(long blonde hair and sailor suit): Francis, was madly taken

with her and followed her everywhere, murmuring in rapture, 'Oh, oh, oh, she smells like the inside of my sponge!'

He also shared my passion for acting and every morning after breakfast we would scurry down to the apple orchard, throw ourselves down on the cold dewy grass and plot out our play for the day, in which, inevitably, I played the prince and Francis played the princess. Violet's suspicions were first aroused when she caught Francis stealing one of her lipsticks, but the crunch came when she spotted him in drag, tied to a tree. After that she put her foot down and thereafter changing sex was forbidden.

Hughie, Guy's youngest son, could hardly have been more different: he liked to slouch around dressed as a gangster: muddy face, slouch hat over one eye and a toy gun. He teamed up with two like-minded village urchins to form a gang known as the Council of Three.

Our Headquarters – The Black Hole [a small shed off the tennis courts]

Our Coat of Arms: Skull and Crossbones.

Our motto: 'Reach for the Skies.'

Our National Anthem: 'Off We Go with the Body in the Bag'.

Our enemies: Francis, Violet and all her smart friends.

Our allies: Joan and Iris (who are *not* smart!).

The signatories to the above were 'Joan Wyndham, Iris Wyndham and Hugh Whindam'.

This sort of thing kept us amused during the day but the evenings were the best time of all. There was wild Apache dancing to the gramophone, sing-songs and all kinds of wonderful games – we loved Charades, dressed in bedspreads and Violet's Paris hats, the scenes ranging from the Bastille to the ballroom, and the Detective Game, with Hughie as a witness – 'I saw her through the keyhole, gloating over alcohol in her boodoor!'

There were also Shakespeare readings, with Violet as Cleopatra curled up on the sofa, her behind in tight trousers well in evidence murmuring, 'To my voluptuousness there is no bottom!' Naturally this got a big laugh, much to Violet's annoyance. My Cleopatra, I have to say, was very much better. I wore a beautiful gold tunic from the dressing-up chest with clusters of white flowers behind my ears and black stuff on my eyelids. I really let myself go and was much praised by the actor Teddy Underdown – he thought I had a real talent for this sort of thing! Oh, Hell! I'm getting far too present indicative. Damned swank, I know, but it's not really, because I know how unutterably wanting I am but I <u>will</u> get through. I <u>will</u>!!'

Three generations. Me, Mummy and Granny, 1922

Mummy and Daddy at Clouds, 1920

Clouds

My great-grandparents, Percy and Madeline Wyndham, on their golden
wedding anniversary at Clouds, 1910

Mummy and Daddy at The Races, 1919

Granny, aged twenty-five, at home in Romania

Granny with Lord French – 'Peter Pan and Wendy', at Phoenix Lodge, Dublin, 1921

Mummy (top right), Sid (top left) and friends acting in a charity show
for East End Settlement

From photograph at the Convent of the Assumption. I am in the second
row from the top, fourth from left

Domestic bliss! At home with Mummy, Sid, Lucky and Jones,
Evelyn Gardens, 1929

Me in the end of term show at RADA, 1937

Mummy and I were sleeping in the little cottage at the end of the garden. Before we retired we always went up to say good night to Wendy, lying as usual in all her anti-ageing paraphernalia – cold cream on her face, pipe-cleaner curlers in her hair, a chin strap tied on top of her head and a little tin circle stuck between her eyebrows to keep out the wrinkles – gazing wistfully at a portrait of Peter Pan on the wall opposite. I, of course, put my foot in it by asking, 'Who's that funny old geezer in the picture?' I was immediately banished upstairs to bed, but took my revenge. I discovered a little crack in the beams just above her bed and found that if I poured a glass of water through it, it fell straight on to her curlers.

I realised that this was a mean thing to do but recently Wendy and I had not been getting on very well. She had a mad idea that I should become a deb and go to some ghastly finishing school called the Monkey Club where you walked around with a book on your head and learnt how to curtsy. She also kept chasing me with her lipstick, trying to make me look posh, when all I wanted was to slop around in shorts and wellies, fishing for caddis worms and tiddlers.

Wendy and Violet, on the other hand, got on famously and had long sessions with their photo-albums, Violet tearing up any photos of my grandmother Minnie, and Granny drawing horns on Pompous Percy.

Back at school, everything seemed a bit flat after the excitements of Orchard Close. There were all the usual worries, exams, rows with nuns and pursuit of our cracks.

Even my mother's letters were a bit uninspiring:

Poor old Jessie has been to the doctor with a swelling on her umbeleikis [sic]. We've also had a plaige of fleas – is that the right spelling? So I bought a few yards of silk from Tullys to make myself a fleabag.

I have ordered your birthday cake from Mrs Deschuyter and told her to put lots of rum in it like last time.

Are you wearing your combinations? Have you put the lining in your coat? It seems to be getting a bit chilly.

Yes [I wrote back], *I have got the lining in my coat, but please don't write about Jessie's 'umbeleikis' again. Shar read your letter and thought it was something rude. I told her it was just some strange kind of fish that Jessie kept but I don't think she believed me. Shar is still being foul to me. The other day she said I was callous and indolent and quite content to remain bad just because I didn't turn a hair when she blew me up at her music lesson. So I promptly let myself go and burst out crying and went on howling to the end of the lesson. She d——n well won't call me unfeeling again!*

The dancing mistress is being changed soon, thank
God, but I'm afraid it's only going to be another gymbag.
PS Send me some Marmite and some blackberry jam –
please.

Then, suddenly, everything changed. For the first time ever we became conscious of the great world outside the convent walls as one exciting drama followed another.

First came the Spanish Civil War, with those horrid Republicans cutting off priests' ears and raping nuns! Franco was our hero, chosen by God to be Spain's saviour. Even my mother's letters became more exciting and now, instead of combs and coat-linings, it was Jews and Fascists fighting in the streets, and 'Have you heard about that wonderful Siege of the Alcazar? It's like something out of medieval days.'

Heard about it? We talked of nothing else, pinching newspapers from the senior common room and gloating over every grisly detail. We read about the brave, starving rebels, holding out for seventy days in the ruined fortress, living on mule stew and stagnant water. Smokers were the worst off, and risked their lives nightly in full view of the snipers to pick mulberry leaves and rose petals that they brought back to make roll-ups.

Down in the catacombs, fetid with rotting corpses, five hundred and fifty women and children lay huddled together, racked with disease. Yet in spite of this the women still took a pathetic pride in their appearance: they manufactured face powder from plaster scraped off the cellar walls, and never let themselves be seen without it. The men, too, put on a brave show, decked out in the uniforms of Napoleonic Hussars, filched from a neighbouring museum. There were, of course, no medical supplies and the doctors amputated limbs with a meat saw.

When Franco finally raised the siege on 27 September we all thronged to church to sing 'Deo Gratias' and treated it like a public holiday. Then, only three months later, there was another drama, this time rather a sad one: the abdication of Edward VIII.

People are saying how wonderfully Mr Baldwin has behaved and how right it was to be firm about this marriage. The new king is said to have given poor little Edward a Scots peerage, I think, but I feel awfully sorry for him and like him much better than that boring old George. All his cracks are going about looking red and damp. As for the nuns, they can talk of nothing else, and last night we were allowed to sit up late to hear the proclamation. Hundreds of people were in tears. I thought his speech was marvellous – just a little bit melodramatic at the end when he said, 'God save the King!' which made me feel rather hysterical, but was super all the same.

Normally by now I would have been looking forward to Christmas with all its fun and games – but, from Mummy's recent letters, it was more likely to be a time of gloom and anxiety:

Poor Granny has fallen off her throne and no mistake – not much of the beautiful Mrs Bennett left now, alas. She is seriously ill but refuses to stay in bed, sitting like an old yellow skeleton, clutching her Japanese scarlet robe about her with a bloodless claw. She is helpless as a child and weeps at the slightest thing. Her mind wanders, taking her back to her Romanian childhood wandering through the woods, and paddling through the streams. She speaks only in Romanian, calling to her 'mamoushka' for help. I think she is going to die.

Before we broke up, I received one more letter:

The doctor thinks she has only a few more weeks. I go and sit with her every evening, feeding her with chicken jelly as she can no longer feed herself. She can hardly speak either, but when she does, it is still always in Romanian. Her hands have gone quite transparent and strangely enough her face has regained some of its early beauty. It has lost that terrible haunted look and now at last, she seems peaceful and happy.

*I am simply harrowed to the bone over it all. Of course
she doesn't realise how ill she is. I have to speak cheerfully
while all the time my throat is sort of closing up. I didn't
think that I should mind so much.*

And so I came home to the worst Christmas of my
life – no presents, no turkey, no tree, just an awful lot of
praying. Aunt Olivia came to stay with us. She didn't seem
too keen on praying but drank an awful lot of whisky.

I wrote in my diary:

When Granny finally died, she went to nothing, her
body was like that of a girl of sixteen. The first time
I was allowed into her bedroom, I saw only a flat
sheet, as if she had flown away, but she was under it,
very pale and lovely, with her hair brushed straight
back like a boy, and the sweetest little chin and neck,
with all the double chin melted away. She had
beautiful bare shoulders, and a look of smiling
triumph on her face like that of the death mask of
the Inconnue de la Seine, but the smile only lasted
a few hours. Soon after, the undertaker arrived,
surprisingly young and chic, with golden curls and
a pearl necklace. Aunt Olivia blundered about in a
vague manner, trying hard to be helpful. 'Of course,
poor darling Dick ought to be doing all this,' she said,

'but then poor darling Dick never did do anything
he ought to have done, did he?'

It has taken me quite a long time to realise that I
shall never see Granny again. What an extraordinary
thought, and how mysterious and unreal this death
seems, like something out of a book of old magic –
a genie who takes people out of this world and makes
them vanish. When I come home next, she will have
left London. She will not have gone to Panama, Paris
or Romania, she will have gone on to another plane –
a strata of space and spirit. If I say, 'Where is
Granny?' they will say she has gone to Elysium,
Nirvana, or Heaven – what you will. She knows now
all that has happened from the beginning of time, she
understands how there can be 'Three in One'. How
wrong it seems connected with someone so prosaic
and worldly as one's grandmother, last seen staggering
out of a shop in Kensington laden with purchases –
potted hyacinths and marron glacés – wearing
galoshes and a fur coat.

We must all pray for the poor old girl. She'll need
it. The awful thing is, I can't say I'm terribly sorry
about it – but she _is_ of my race and clan, I have her
blood in me and I ought to pray for the soul of a
relative even when she has been a bore and a sorrow to
us all her life.

Granny was not very well off, but all that she had she left to Iris, who now could buy a *real* car, not one that had to be tied up with string. But her biggest extravagance was a small thatched cottage, set in a cowfield with a small stream running past it. This, of course, meant fewer visits to Orchard Close.

I shall miss Francis and Hughie, the smart young men and the endless evening games – also the cottage where we stayed, with its water tank full of squiggly pink worms that I could feed to my fish, the rats in the thatch and the white owl in the pear tree. But our new cottage has one great advantage – a little log cabin at the bottom of the garden which Mummy has promised me shall be <u>mine</u>!

I couldn't wait to see it and bombarded her with questions:

What colour are the curtains, and what colour have you painted the gramophone? What flowers are in the window boxes? Is the stream bathable in or do horrible things bite your toes? One thing that's very important. I'd like more than anything else to have my own cupboard with my very own tea-set in it. Then I could ask you to tea sometimes and feel as if I'm a grown-up and have a house of my very own.

My questions were soon answered:

*The curtains are white with blue flowers on them and I
have painted the gramophone red – the flowers in the
window box are that word I can't spell – 'nurstursiums'.
Of course you can have your own tea-things. The stream is
bathable but a bit horrific. I bathe in the company of frogs
and caddis worms with mayflies sitting on my shoulders.
The only thing that worries me is that the church is much
too far away, even to bicycle to. I spoke to a priest when I
went to confession the other day and he said it would be
quite all right for us to say Sunday prayers at home. It
would be even lovelier if we could find a secret place in
the woods, make our own little chapel there. We could
nail a crucifix to a tree and light a little fire to burn incense
on. We would, of course, keep it secret and not let anyone
know.*

Over the next few months the cottage slowly took
shape, and became a magical place for both of us. Only Sid
remained uninvolved, having no interest whatsoever in the
country. Iris tried in vain to convert her to the joys of
Nature:

*I make her plant seeds, and water them (very unwillingly). I
ask her to walk with me at night, slowly, smelling any good*

scents there are – often, I fear, only pussy cats! I have
made her read The Wind in the Willows *and examine*
such fascinating things as cuckoo spits, ladybirds and
spiders' webs but her mind is always on something else
like her forthcoming lecture on Communism to students of
Bedford College.

Of course Iris still loved Sid, but the gap between them
was slowly widening. She would find strange scraps of
paper lying around: 'Never eat when you're hungry. Never
drink when you're thirsty. Always sit up straight in your
chair and never lean back!' For Iris, who loved her creature
comforts, this was all a bit worrying.

Sid's visits to the cottage were rare, and Iris often
found herself alone there. Then one day she met a friend
of Sid's called Marilyn, who became her 'cottage
friend'. She not only kept Iris company but also loved
the natural things Iris loved. A letter from my mother to
'my dearest Marilyn', written soon after her first visit,
expresses it all:

You just don't know how lovely it is to share all my little
interests with you, entering into and really enjoying the
things I have had, for so long, to keep to myself. I've never
known anyone who entered so fully into all those funny
little things that amuse and enchant me. For instance

when I tell you that a sparrow brought two babies to my table this morning and fed them on cake crumbs, I know that you will be interested! Also, I long to show you the sticklebacks' nest – the male guards it all day long and fights off any fish that come near. There's so much I want to tell you about that I've decided to keep a cottage diary, just in case I forget some of it.

Monday. *Today, a little chaffinch made friends with me. He came into the sitting room and let me stroke him, and now he is waiting for me outside the front door!*

Tuesday. *A mole has heaved himself up into the middle of our seed bed and, since the rain, the lawn is crawling with slugs. Last night, I went out with a torch and caught them eating my beans!*

Thursday. *Woken early by a terrific burst of birdsong – the cuckoo included. The sun was out so I went into the garden and it was like an enchanted world. So many new things have come up. The first sweet peas, the first wild roses and night-scented stock. The hay is being carried past the cottage and everything smells like heaven. The nest in the honeysuckle has five eggs, white with brown smudges, and I can hear flutterings near the gate where the thrush has her nest. I think they must be nearly ready to fly.*

And then, after a blissful summer together, they fell in love and 'my dearest Marilyn' became 'my darling little banana squirrel', signed 'Iris squirrel'. Where the banana came from, I couldn't say.

And on the rare occasions that Marilyn had to go back to London, Iris wrote her passionate letters:

> *My precious one,*
> *Come back soon. I want to share <u>everything</u> with you.*
> *You are so full of love, that even now when you are away,*
> *I feel it all around me. You leave it behind you, hidden in*
> *the cottage cushions, in the warm shadows of the trees. A*
> *beautiful red poppy has suddenly burst out of its bud in the*
> *sun and is shining across the garden. I shall welcome you*
> *back with such happiness, my darling little <u>tiny</u> banana!*

A stranger reading these letters would probably think they were having a full-blown lesbian relationship, but I knew better: I often stayed with them and always went up to kiss my mother goodnight. She looked so cosy and happy in her hand-knitted pink bedjacket with her bar of Bournvita chocolate, a glass of milk and the latest Agatha Christie. Did I really think that, as soon as I left, she would chuck Agatha to the floor, leap out of bed and hare down the corridor to jump on the peacefully snoring Marilyn? No, their love was passionate but it was also pure. A rare combination.

Luckily, Sid was not at all jealous as she and Marilyn were such old friends. It was the ideal set-up: Sid and Marilyn loved Iris, and loved each other; Iris loved both of them, and all three loved God.

It was my last year at school, and cracks were now a thing of the past. Even John Gielgud had been replaced by another Hamlet – the totally gorgeous Laurence Olivier. I was still running around with the Bitchum Whorums, and reasonably happy, but I missed Anne D. terribly. She had left to go on to drama school, so I was left without a best friend, everyone else having paired off, and there was no one with whom I could share secrets or discuss the facts of life. Mother Damien was still keen on me, and actually gave me a sex talk: telling me that there was something called the safe period. I asked Mummy about this and she said there was no such thing, unless, perhaps, just before good old Alex, 'but if I were you, I wouldn't count on it'.

Sodalities are the big excitement at the moment – you start off as an Innocent, become an Angel and end gloriously as an 'Enfant de Marie', a 'Child of Mary' with a medal hung round your neck on a beautiful blue satin ribbon. Last year I was made an Angel and there was a wonderful beano afterwards. Unfortunately the nuns rather spoilt it, by lurking behind us and pretending to feel our imaginary wings, just as we were reaching for another slice of cake.

But this term comes the final test – will we or won't we be considered holy enough to become Children of Mary? I and the three other Bitchum Whorums are all on the list and the nuns are voting this week. Shar, of course, certainly won't vote for me as she considers me a corrupting influence. She also claims that when she asks me to do something, I obey, but only in a sulky and ungracious fashion. This is a lie! I have put myself out lately several times to do her loathsome behest with a cheerful face. Also, she doesn't think much of my character because of the slouchy way I walk, if you please! So, she concludes, I won't get in for an E. de M. . . .

However, this morning when the lists went up, she received a large and substantial <u>raspberry</u>, for I alone got in out of all the four of us. Poor Edie, who is much holier than me, is in floods. God <u>knows</u> how I got in. It is really wicked to be the only one of us four, for I am much worse than they are – however there it is.

I'm afraid you will have to fork out some dough [I wrote to Mummy]. *There is a medal, five shillings – a chain,*

*three and sixpence, ribbon, tenpence, and E. de M. picnic,
two and sixpence, so it looks like a little matter of eleven
and tenpence, Chérie!*

*I was also a bit worried about some of the awful things
that I had heard you might have to do if you were a Child
of Mary. I tackled a priest about it and as soon as I could
get him off Birth Control and the seduction of Irish servant
girls, I laid the E. de M. problem before him, and told
him that although I wanted to be Our Lady's child, I had
no vocation for the Sodality side of it and therefore didn't
think I ought to be one. Whereupon he put a completely
new and sensible point of view before me. Apparently it
was enough just to be underneath Our Lady's special
protection and there was no need to join in parish
activities, visit hospitals and rush around to Whist Drives
if you don't like that sort of thing. In fact it is enough if it
is purely an inward and spiritual sort of thing. I said I still
thought that would be a rather dirty trick, and a one-sided
bargain, but he assured me that it was all right and that
the things I have mixed feelings over are not part of the
Sodality at all, just trivialities that have grown up around
it. So I agreed that if that was so, there was nothing to
prevent me being one.*

Shar, of course, was furious and longed to find an
excuse for humiliating me. Unfortunately it was my

mother who unwittingly gave her the perfect chance. Knowing that she was in charge of drama, she wrote to her asking her what she thought of RADA and, even worse, her opinion of my chance of becoming an actress. Our end-of-term play was to be *A Midsummer Night's Dream* and I, to my delight, was to play Titania. My fairy friends and I rehearsed every evening in the garden, swooping around on our imaginary wings and occasionally tripping over my pet tortoises. I knew in my heart that I was good, and each rehearsal was more rewarding than the last.

Then, one day, I was summoned to Shar's office. 'Well, Joan,' she said, 'we have been discussing your performance and I'm afraid that you're not quite our idea of a Fairy Queen. For a start, you're far too big and you have this awful slouching walk with your tummy sticking out. What we really need is someone small and delicate. Heather Bell, perhaps.' *Heather Bell?* The ugliest girl in the school? 'Still,' Shar continued, 'we don't want to disappoint your mother, do we, so we thought you might play Hyppolita.' Well, I thought, forcing back my tears, that's not *too* bad. At least I've got a couple of good scenes. Then two weeks later, Shar summoned me again: 'You know, of course, that Peggy, our head girl, is unfortunately leaving this term. Well, we thought it would be only fair to give her a nice farewell present. So we have decided to let *her* play Hyppolita and you can be her lady-in-waiting.'

If Shar thought she was going to kill my acting ambitions, she had another think coming. I might have felt like sobbing and screaming but I controlled myself and vowed that, one day, I would be a flaming star with my name in lights, if only to say yah-boo-sucks to you, horrible old Shar.

But first, of course, I had to learn to act. Mummy had just told me that before I could be accepted by RADA, I would have to take my school certificate, 'whatever *that* is'.

So I studied in bed every night by the light of my E. de M. candle, stuck into the top of an Odo-Ro-No bottle. Blasphemy? Sometimes I worked hard all night, still fully dressed, and rolled out of bed in the morning in time for breakfast.

English and history were going well, but my French was a bit shaky so Mummy decided I should spend the next hols with a family in Versailles and attend language classes at a nearby college. I had never been out of England before, so I was terribly excited. As the train passed through the Normandy countryside, I sat glued to the window.

It all looked ten times nicer than England, *[I wrote in my diary]*. Greener, brighter and more picturesque as if everything was posing for its picture. All around were fields and flowering apple trees, frightfully green grass full of daisies, and glorious cows, very white with shiny black spots. Also dazzling white geese with coral beaks, clean fleecy goats and long-legged foals, all gambolling together under the blossoms. They looked as if they had been newly painted – so theatrical that they were almost unreal, like pictures in a fairy book.

At the station there were many blue-jawed brigands, with berets dead straight on their heads and women with shawls and bedroom slippers. The porters were quite different from the English, very young and spending most of their time kissing each other loudly on both cheeks, or kicking each other's behinds.

When I reached the house where I and my room-mate were to stay, I was met in the hall by Madame, in a long shawl with a huge cameo brooch, her hair piled up on her head, very regal, but surprisingly with bright red fingernails.

She seems to me to be a decent old girl *[I wrote to my mother]*. Papa is very sweet with little brown monkey eyes, a huge curling moustache and a flowing black silk cravat. He travels everywhere 'en bicyclette'.

The house is full of chandeliers, stuffed birds and aspidistras. Apparently, my room-mate and I are allowed to smoke and go out into the town by ourselves because as Madame says we are 'serieuse' and not like some. However, she warns us not to let ourselves be kissed by 'des Arabes ou des Soldats'.

To reach our room we have to climb six dark worm-eaten flights of stairs, smelling of garlic. The room itself is hideous with dreadful wallpaper and a picture of the Crucifixion over my bed. My room-mate is a bouncing girl from Reading who says her prayers every night, wears woollen underwear and eats sausages in bed. She is very nice indeed.

As one bed has worse light and a ceiling you bump your head on, we are going to change over halfway through. I am lying in bed eating a delicious 'grosse bouchée'. The maid has just put her head around the door to say, 'There will be no hot water today because it is Jeudi.' What the hell has Jeudi got to do with hot water?

Now I know why they call the French mean. There is no ink in the ink wells, no water in the carafes and there are no baths. We are only allowed a sink with cold water. There is no door to it and Monsieur's room is directly opposite, with only a curtain between us and Papa, so we don't wash at all! Even the solitary cold tap in our room is turned off during the day, to make quite sure we can't waste water by washing our hands.

Dinner is a long drawn-out affair with seven

courses! There is a little silver rack beside each plate and I found to my disgust we are supposed to put our dirty knives and forks on it and use them again for the next course and the next! No salad bowls are provided so we have to dunk our lettuce into the cold gravy. During the meal, Madame addresses remarks to each of us in turn. We try to look intelligent and say 'oui' or 'non' in the right places. Papa eats practically the whole of his meal off the point of his knife, and once he is finished, he entertains us with his favourite hunting songs, 'la chasse' being his passion. There are only two things one must be careful not to mention. One is Monsieur Blum, the leader of the Popular Front. The very mention of his name makes Madame spit and cry 'Blum! Rouge. Rouge. Rouge!' The other is 'les Juifs' who are apparently the enemies of humanity, the perpetrators of every abomination under the sun. I must also remember to refer to the Jeyes as 'La Tante Fannée'.

After dinner we have to shake hands with Papa, be kissed on both cheeks by Maman and then up to bed where we have a riotous time pretending we are two cocottes, Queenie and Flossie. We both have our favourite customers. Mine is called Raoul, with green eyes and red hair. I also read a lot in bed. I have finished my horror book and am starting on old

Shakespeare yet again.

Sunday All the family's relations are here today
including their seven-year-old niece, Stephanie. She has
a wonderful vocabulary for her age. Just now I splashed
her with water and she called me 'sale derrière du
cochon'. Most of her time is spent petting an ageing
malevolent cat called Fifi which the family adore and
treat like an elder daughter.

Wednesday The day we finally got to see Paris. I think it
is simply lovely. London is bum compared with it. The
boulevards were crowded with good-looking men and
chic women. Even the old hags had their eyebrows a
mere thread with thick coatings of rouge under their
moustaches. Why do so many French women have
moustaches, I wonder?

Thursday At last I've started attending lectures at a
nearby university. It is a rather frightening place with a
communal dining hall. When some English greenhorn
ventures in wearing a hat, about two hundred students
start to bang their spoons on their glasses, shouting
'Chap-eau!' in unison until the wretched girl guesses
that they mean her.

Saturday The French students gave a dance for the English visitors. A very gay affair with champagne at fourpence a glass (a rather shady vintage known as 'Veuve Muriel'). The minute I walked in, I was swept off my feet by a young student called Jean Bernard who taught me a wild dance called La Java. We danced all night to accordions and violins – funny little jigging tunes, the most popular at the moment being 'Café au lait au lit'. Since then Jean has taken me under his wing completely. He is twenty-one, very pleasant looking, wears corduroy trousers and studies philosophy. He also likes Bach, Baudelaire and 'Le Jazz Hot' – altogether, he is 'à mon goût'.

Wednesday My room-mate fell violently in love with a boy at this dance. She keeps bewailing that she is not glamorous so I got to work on her with scent and Max Factor makeup and she is hoping that he will soon come to the point, whatever <u>that</u> may mean.

Today, Jean took me to a fair at Montmartre. Everything from fire-eating cannibals to Russians on motor bikes riding the Wall of Death. We walked along happily, eating wild strawberries and pieces of fresh coconut and rode on the Dodgem cars. I loved the crowd, the dust, the blazing music, the clowns and the *awful* women who threw their skirts in the air when they danced.

In the evening, we ate at a café bar in the quarter, a place for workmen where, for five shillings, we had beefsteak garni, fried potatoes and a salad with a dressing that was out of this world, followed by éclairs, stewed plums and excellent liqueurs. For company, we had a huge melancholy dog and a lean cat that kept its hopeful nose on my knees throughout the meal. I loved the paper tablecloths – they're great for scribbling on.

Jean is very old for his age, very intelligent and of quite extraordinary sensitivity. Every night we walk in the park and sit under the trees talking – sometimes till after midnight. But sex has not yet reared its ugly head! Jean is of a subtlety and tact that is quite unbelievable. He has not even tried to kiss me yet. On the other hand, he can express more with a caress of his fingertips than most men can with their whole body.

Saturday Went shopping in a kind of happy daze, scent, makeup, silk stockings and wonderful clothes, all much cheaper than in England. I even bought a black mantilla to wear in the evening and a pair of huge white earrings. Maman told me that only a 'poule' [a tart] would wear such earrings, but I don't care. I've found that French men don't bother you much on the streets. So far nobody has pinched my bottom though there was one chap who tried to hire me for his brothel

('What you say? I give you good chance! Good money!'). I found the safest thing was to keep my eyes to myself as looks can be misinterpreted. Look too closely at a soldier and he'll think you're expecting a kiss, admire some mangy pariah dog and the owner will think that you want to buy it.

Watch out, too, when crossing the road as the French are totally reckless drivers and a taxi ride in Paris is one long list of hair's breadth escapes. Nevertheless, any drawbacks they may have are more than made up for by the easy-going friendliness of everyone I have met. In the tram yesterday, a very fat woman who was standing next to me shoved a basket full of radishes onto my lap and said, 'Hold these, Mignon, while I do up my suspenders.' I can't imagine this happening in England!

In the evening we went to the local cinema, a very low joint indeed. Sat in the best seats, price ninepence, 'attrappéd' three fleas between the two of us and saw Eisenstein's film *Ivan the Terrible*.

On our return, Maman told us that the time had come for our monthly bath and, to our delight, we saw hot water for the first time. This was just as well as my belated curse had suddenly descended on me during the Russian film as it often does when I get too excited!

Monday Blum has given a general holiday today and there are great Communist demonstrations everywhere. All the reds in town, thousands of them, are going in procession through the streets, carrying banners, shouting, singing and waving their fists in the air in the red salute. Lots of them were drunk and various young girls were behaving in an abandoned manner all over the road. A man with a red money box came up to me and waved it under my nose shouting, 'Pour les martyres de l'assassin Franco!' This kind of thing went on all day.

Tuesday Everything has now quietened down so we thought we'd better take in a bit of culture. We started off at Notre Dame looking in amazement at the gargoyles. There is one putting out its tongue at Paris and another eating the backside of a dog. It seems a funny idea to put such utterly evil and revolting creatures on the front of a church. Then came the Château of Versailles but it was all rather boring. There were two soldiers in the crowd and when they passed a picture of Louis XVI, they first looked round to see that no one was watching and then saluted it in a rather embarrassed fashion. I wonder why?

Next day, we did the Louvre, and were dragged around dreary picture salons. I had to shut my eyes most of the time and whenever I lifted them, I winced

and turned pale at some fresh monstrosity. All the
early stuff was OK, but I couldn't stand the period of
pseudo-classicism. All those fat women in Grecian
tunics with one bosom uncovered. Rubens, in
particular, made me so cross. They were all frightfully
'volupté' and sentimental but with *nothing* in them. All
the sculpture sections were marvellous, especially the
Greek, but I didn't have time to see them properly as
we spent so long snooping round those stinking
pictures. As for the Eiffel Tower I think it's the ugliest
thing in Paris.

Friday For three days now there has been no paper in
the Tante Fannée. I've had to use all the tissue paper
from my trunk.

Luckily, I have been asked to dinner by my
Romanian relatives in Paris. They are very grand and
rich so I will probably be able to pinch a few rolls of
paper to take home with me. I arrived at tea-time and
there, assembled on the terrace, was a most formidable
array of Comtesses, Marquesas and I don't know what,
all in outrageously smart hats, sipping tea from egg-
shell china and dipping genteelly into a vast bowl of
whipped cream sprinkled with cinnamon. I advanced
nervously, feeling all shiny nose, large feet and dropped
hem. I was far too shy to do justice to the magnificent

spread. Finally my cousin Nicky took pity on me and introduced me to the assembled snobs as his cousin 'Jern Weedham', and once they realised I was one of the tribe, everybody was frightfully nice to me. With my confidence totally restored, I was now able to cope with an immensely rich dinner which went on for hours. We started with lobster, cooked in wine, butter and cream, and ended with fraises des bois and peaches in whipped cream, all washed down with white Alsatian wine and Curaçao. I'm afraid I got a little bit drunk, so was glad to stay the night, going home in the morning with my handbag stuffed with paper for the Tante Fannée.

On my last night, the whole family gathered round the grand piano for a sing-song. It was a bit boring really as they only seemed to like songs about war or revolution – 'The Marseillaise', 'Sombre et Meuse', 'La Brabançonne' and 'The Carmagnole'. I was longing to say a last goodbye to Jean but all my attempts were thwarted. He was the very first boy I'd ever been out with and I'm going to miss him like hell.

I have now reached my last term at school:

Exams are going well but there's something else that bothers me. After all these years, genuflecting, fasting

and praying, I'm afraid I'm beginning to lose my faith.
I remember the very first time I had doubts – could
Jesus really have risen from the grave? Then I
remembered how Mary Magdalen had mistaken him
for the gardener, and I thought surely no one could
have invented *that*! In any case, I still love Jesus, and
think him the most wonderful man who ever lived. It's
God that gives me the pip.

In the great white dawn of life's history, *He* was
there, all-good, all-knowing and all-powerful, the ball
at his feet and no other players on the field. So what
made him create the Devil? Did he need someone to
kick the ball back to him? Having created a totally
good universe, why did he need to turn it into a
battleground for good and evil? Maybe he found an
all-good universe too boring. Not enough fun, not
enough kudos, no competition?

Or perhaps the Manichean heretics were right –
God was the original schizophrenic, combining good
and evil within himself, like the black and white stripes
of a child's humbug.

And where did *we* come in?? Why did he need us?
And why, after giving us a brief taste of happiness,
did he condemn us to lifetimes of endless pain and
sorrow? What did we do to deserve this? Or, as
Adam might have said, 'I ate the apple, but who

planted the tree?' Sometimes I can't help feeling pity for him. Imagine having the whole world on your conscience.

But even after Adam and Eve had left Eden and settled down to a normal family life, God still had to interfere and set the stage for the first real sin – murder. No nun has ever told us why Cain killed Abel. I have only found out by accident, opening the Bible at random. Apparently God, after setting an angel with a flaming sword at the gates of Paradise, paid the occasional neighbourly call on Eve and their sons Cain and Abel. One day he arrived demanding a special present. Abel, in charge of the animals, brought him a fat haunch of meat, but Cain who tilled the fields, could only manage a basketful of his choicest crops. God – obviously no vegetarian – praised Abel's gift to the skies but turned up his nose scornfully at Cain's offering. Deeply humiliated, Cain, in a fit of rage, killed Abel. Man's first murder but surely God's responsibility?

Ask a Jesuit and he'll bang on about the beauty of free will and the choice between good and evil. Why not a choice between good and better? I ask myself. Why should we be sacrificed as a burnt offering to tickle God's nose with the sweet smell of repentance?

For me, the screams of one innocent and uncomprehending child wipe out all the good deeds ever done. Did God's coming to Earth and his crucifixion compensate for their suffering? No! He couldn't even manifest himself in a sinful human body like ours but had to be conceived 'immaculately', with the Holy Ghost stepping in just to make sure poor Joseph didn't throw a spanner into the works with a touch of the old Adam. Otherwise he might have known what the odds are like – to be born into a corrupt body, landed with that old joker Free Will, and then set to walk the tightrope between Heaven and Hell.

Of course, we don't *have* to believe anyone is damned – only Judas. Poor bloody Judas, the only man to be damned before he was even born. Of course it was all pre-arranged. That great passion play – don't believe it wasn't well planned and rehearsed from way back. And some poor mug had to play the Judas role. The leading man, of course, was already cast!

Do you know, you're talking all the time like someone who actually believes in it all? That's the horror of it, not being able to dismiss it all as a bloodstained farce! For after all, if there *is* a God, and he arranged his universe in such a way that innocents

shall suffer, at least it means that he is there to take
them to his bosom and make it up to them when they
die – but if there's nothing, no God, no Heaven, and
they suffer just the same with no one to comfort them,
nothing but a cold dark void into which they fall, then
the whole thing is meaningless. Better even a cruel
schizophrenic God than no arms for their broken
bodies to fall into.

And so it went on. One day believing, the next not
believing. A few weeks later, on a 'belief day' I wrote in
my diary about Hell:

Just a kind of limbo with no flames or devils. What
makes it into your personal Hell is the fact that when
you die you are shown what God is like. If during
your life, you chose him then you will get him. If
not, not. But once having seen him, to be without
him *is* Hell. The way a woman will live in perfect
happiness with her middle-aged husband but after
one night with a slim and expert stranger, she realises
what she is missing and her life becomes Hell.

As for Heaven, I see it as a place with no angels, just
all the people you have loved in your life. I might even
meet Jesus there and be relieved to find that he was just
a normal little boy, a carpenter's son, and no relation to

147

that grim-faced fellow on the golden throne with a
ghostly bird sitting on his head.

My last day at school finally arrived.

The eternal holidays loom ahead, all of us exchanging
addresses and telephone numbers, although we know
we may never use them. How sad it seems. Five long
years of friendship and intimacy all vanished in a flash.
Of course my very best friend Anne Dawson has
already left and gone to RADA, lucky swine! Maybe
one day soon I'll be joining her there.

I am truly sorry to say goodbye to dear Damien,
but delighted to be rid of the odious Shar. In her
farewell lecture to me she complained that I spent far
too much time sitting in the library reading instead of
running after the nuns carrying their holy books or
kneeling all day in the chapel at prayer. In fact I am
delighted to be going home for good away from this
unreal place with its Victorian values which my soul
revolts against. *They* think it's the whole world but *I*
know better!

I naturally imagined that home would be the same as
always, warm and comforting, and my darling mother just

as loving and understanding as ever. I was looking forward to our first meal together. It was sure to be something delicious, a special treat, but to my dismay, my mother explained, 'We are leading the simple life nowadays, so as to have more money to give to the poor,' and produced a meal of *mamaliga*, a kind of Romanian porridge, cabbage soup and apples with mousetrap cheese and black bread to follow.

She hardly ever sees Marilyn or goes to the cottage any more. She is *obsessed* with charity work. She and Sid have their own special charity – the 'Loaves and Fishes', designed to give help to impoverished gentlefolk. The older helpers are called Sprats, I am just a Minnow and the suffering gentlefolk are known as Seahorses. The Sprats' main object is to catch Mackerels – that is, rich patrons. Father Corato, the Holy Halibut, is there to cater to their spiritual needs.

Soon after I came home, they had a meeting, and all the Seahorses arrived promptly in time for tea, including many familiar faces: Penniless Peter, Dreary Ethel and Hungry Helen. After the Viota iced cakes and Marmite sandwiches were all finished, they gave a talk and described recent achievements – a poor man saved from the bailiffs and a companion found for a lonely widow.

149

In case they should run out of distressed gentlefolk, the Sprats also support a House of Hospitality in the East End. It is run by young Catholic workers who give food and shelter to tramps and the unemployed. This is the charity that I like best. The house is untidy and dirty beyond description yet with an atmosphere of peace and the standing-still of time that I have never felt before. I love it because it is so casual and unconventional. You are called by your Christian name as soon as you meet someone. The boys' rooms are a glorious chaos of books and posters, toothpaste, razors and dirty clothes, all heaped in piles on the floor. Father Peter, the young priest who runs the house, often sits with the boys, smoking his pipe, reading them stories from the Bible and stroking a small black kitten on his lap. I'm not allowed to go there too often, in case I never want to leave it! It's such a small, dark, delicious, dirty house!

The only awful thing about Mum and Sid's charities were the shows they put on to raise money – but always with them as the stars. At one particularly excruciating performance, the sight of my mother teetering across the stage in a pink tutu but still wearing her glasses was too much for me and I had to seek refuge in the Jeyes to stifle my giggles, so I decided to take her to a real ballet and show her how lovely it was when properly done.

The Ballets Russes were performing at Covent Garden, so off we went to see *Les Sylphides* with Baronova.

We had very grand seats in the stalls. The audience was a mixed bunch – next to us, there was an old balletomane eating a pear in a juicy manner and in front was a fat dowager, complete with ermine, black pearls and gigolo. The orchestra struck up, and I suddenly felt I could never be happier than just then. The moment seemed to crystallise itself, the thrilling music, the glowing, gilded ceiling, the mass of attentive heads like pebbles under water in the faint greenish glare of the Exit lights, the smell of the old man's pear. Then the crack of light in the curtain, spreading to reveal the stage and the posed ballerina.

She was partnered by Lifar, passionate as a flame, incredibly magnetic yet at the same time as full of bounce as a puppy, as pert as a sparrow and as artless and naïve as a child. I clutched Mummy's arm in ecstasy, my eyes fixed on his Byzantine profile, full, firm buttocks and the lurch of his beautiful young body. Oh, God, I think I'd better stop. (I'll say you had!!!)

In the last minutes of *L'Après-midi*, his body was curved 'bee-wise' over the nymph's veil then the slow descent, the fluttering hands clutching the rock. He really suggested the masturbation of the last moment. God, how he enchants me. His only problem is he dances with his mouth open.

A week later:

Sid is still interested in charity work but has also developed a passionate interest in converting people. She can't stand the idea that our best friend Henry is still not a Catholic. The other night she suddenly pointed a finger in his direction and shouted, 'That man is mine – and I will have him!' Henry, however, is far more interested in his good friend Bertie – the two of them often treat us to their famous impersonation of Wagner's Rhinemaidens with much writhing around on the carpets.

I'd hoped that now I had left school I might see more of my father but he never turned up, and was always late with the maintenance. Sadly, I knew that my mother still loved him. 'When I am in bed,' she confided to me, 'my favourite "think" is still the desert island and Dick striding out of the sea as the sun sets, his shoulders wet and glistening, to lie with me under the palm trees. Lately, I've been making some improvements. I've built myself a lovely little house at the top of a big tree. It is very cosy with a slung hammock and on the ground beneath there is a river and waterfall where I can swim. You've no idea how blissfully I cleave the water in my dreams. Now that you are older, you can come and visit me. I would see you as a grown-up of my own age and we could both have visitors!'

Sunday, gloomy Sunday But Sid's nice friend Sandy arrived after lunch to lighten the gloom. He has taken up broadcasting and done some of the advertisements – 'Uncle Sandy will now tell you how the acid in your stomach could burn a hole in the carpet', or 'Eno's Fruit Salts present the adventures of Mr, Mrs and Master Can't'.

1 October I'm reading a lot at present and have just finished *Mademoiselle de Maupin*. The very peak and essence of beautiful sensuality. In fact, like nothing I have ever read before – a wholly new and completely satisfying experience. I'm also re-painting my room. It is now cream with an orange ceiling.

Tuesday 5th How disgusting men are! The first two nights I go out alone in the dark, I am accosted both times. The first night, walking down the Fulham Road, my hat off and my coat flapping open, a tall, soldierly man with a waxed moustache and green pork pie hat, passes me, and says, with no preliminary in a low, almost expressionless voice, as if it were a well-worn formula: 'Didn't I meet you at Hammersmith Palais de Danse last night?'

'No! I've never been there in my life.'

Next night, I purposely kept my hat on, coat firmly closed, and tried to walk primly. But passing World's End, I heard heavy feet following me from one of the pubs. I crossed the road. A man comes padding after me. I am petrified, waiting for him to speak. At last it comes in a Cockney voice: 'You in service, love?'

'No.'

'Going to the pictures?'

'No.'

'How about tomorrow night, huh?'

You leprous swine, I thought, breaking into a run. He followed me all the way up to my garden gate and eyed it meaningfully. 'Number seven, eh?'

I banged the gate in his face. God, it makes me so furious. I felt like screaming, 'No! I'm *not* in service, I *won't* go to the pictures. You're a lot of whoremongers! I'd like to kick you in a place you won't forget!' What frightened me most was the offhand expressionless tone of their voices, using a special language they were very used to. I felt as if the lid had been lifted from London, showing the darkness underneath.

Next night, *Macbeth* was on the wireless, so I got out of playing ping-pong with Lady Orpen and lay on the sofa, listening to it. Halfway through, I suddenly remembered that that horrible man knew where I lived and I began to be terrified. I imagined him picking the lock of the back door and stealing in so I piled chairs against the door. I lay there talking to myself in a high-pitched hysterical voice. I sounded so good that I acted out the whole of the dagger scene while the terror was still on me. The bravest thing I did that night was go down to the basement and feed the dog.

11 October As a special birthday treat I was taken to see Ram Gopal who has been called the Indian Nijinsky. He is a dream, exquisitely made and a perfect dancer. His Eagle was a golden trembling glory, the most convincing impression of wings I have ever seen on the stage. There was also a blue, glittering peacock dance, but the most exciting of all was his Storm God. The music stops on the crest of a climax and the dancer quivers like a dynamo from head to foot, his bare feet thudding on the stage like thunder while his shaken anklet bells sound like torrential rain.

12 October I have discovered something called the Ballet Club where the Ballet Rambert performs every Sunday night in the little Mercury Theatre. Very small, very cosy. By luck, the first night I was there, they featured the divine Bobby Helpmann. His face may be a bit fish-like but, gosh, what a bottom! I'm not saying that I judged his performance by it, of course, but he certainly has the most divinely made bottom on a man I've seen in a long time.

Madame Rambert sits on the floor in the centre aisle, with her feet straight out in front of her like a gnome. She is tiny, with her hair done up on top of her head and wrapped in white lace. When she tires of the floor, she uses a shooting stick. She mumbles and grunts at bad dancers, or cheers and shouts for her favourites. This makes it a bit difficult for her when her daughter is on stage as she tends to dance like a football captain taken with the gripes in the middle of the big match.

1 November Took Mummy to the Ballet Club. We sat very near the stage, and when Bobby Helpmann made his first superb entrance in *Masques*, I could feel Mummy sit up with a jerk and positively drink in every movement with her mouth hanging open. 'Quelle finesse,' she murmured voluptuously, as she swayed towards the footlights. When the interval came, she staggered out in a daze, made straight for the bar and ordered a G and T. All the way home, she was in an ecstasy, moving her hips and behaving in a most unusual way. This is a side of her I have never seen before.

Sunday 20th Much to my relief, Mummy wasn't free so I went to the Club with Sid and Henry. He was standing in the foyer when Bobby came in with 'boyfriend'. Henry said in his calm, slightly surprised voice, 'My God, what queers!' then looking at Bobby, 'That man's just like a fish!' Me: 'Watch out, Henry. The one in black tights is Mummy's crush. She absolutely worships him.' 'Well, I never thought Iris would fall off the deep end for *anyone* – but that she should go off it for a haddock!'

Wednesday A new excitement has entered our lives. Our Romanian cousin, Nicky, has come over with King Karol of Romania and called after dinner. He is just as charming as he was in Paris, only twenty-nine, the image of Rudolph Valentino, very interesting, amusing, and doesn't mind what he does. He is my second cousin and the only relation I've met so far who I ever want to meet again. He's taking us to the theatre on Saturday, stalls, evening dress, chocolates, taxi there and back. Crumbs! I shall enjoy doing the thing in style for once.

Saturday We saw a play called *Bobby Get Your Gun* with
Gertrude Niessen who sang 'Rhythm Is My Romeo' in
a tight silver dress. Afterwards we went as promised to
the Savoy. We got a table, and me and Nicky had live
oysters with a mound of ice in the middle and they
squirmed when you squeezed some lemon on to them.
After that we had chicken and asparagus and drank
champagne rosé. After dinner there was a cabaret show
with dagos doing the most miraculous leaps and
distortions. And then Nicky danced with me and
madness got into my blood.

I had never danced cheek to cheek with a man
before, only with convent girls. I take back anything
I've ever said against modern dancing. It is the most
thrilling and satisfying thing I've ever experienced.
Nicky dances beautifully – like a doped panther, only
not so doped, either! He holds you very close. You feel
the movements and interplay of his muscles against
your body and move like one person. If I was writing a
novelette I should say, 'We drifted like souls a-swoon
to the sobbing of saxophones.' He seemed to flatter
you in every way with his every touch and movement.

The rhythm made me feel drugged and I understand
now why the church says 'immodest dances'. I couldn't
think why, before. Of course – they satisfy every
appetite and sensual instinct of our animal nature. I

used to think once that I could never even let a man kiss me and as for sleeping with one – it would be a mad impossibility, contrary to nature. Now I know there is nothing my nature could not be capable of. Neither immorality, murder nor even unnatural vice. I could love for their bodies, and sometimes for their souls, an infinite number of men at the same time. I think I would make an ideal whore, but my religious upbringing bars me from such things. That only, for I have none of that salutary horror of sin that priests speak of. In fact I can think of at least six men I know that drive me to a passion of desire when I am in their presence. Is this unnatural? I've never met other women who felt like this. It's the convent's fault. They repressed me for nearly ten years with the result that my friends and I talked vile filth all day. Also I am my father's child. Maybe I was happier sewing altar cloths while Mother Editha read from *Fabiola, the Roman Martyr* or the story of the chaste Cecilia who died of modesty – but perhaps not. One was out of temptation there, but my God it was dull. As for Cecilia, I guess one has to be born that way.

Then I received a wonderful birthday present from Mummy. She agreed to let me study at RADA in the new year! Of course I had to audition for a place, and was coached with a group of others by a fat, middle-aged man named West. Shattered by my first rehearsal of *Mädchen in Uniform* with him, I wrote in my diary,

There's no getting away from it. Old West is a 'ham'. He goes too far, wanting more emotion than is possible without over-acting. We all got worked up and hysterical – I nearly died when I had to clasp him round the waist, while he delivered himself in the most overpowering way of 'It is wrong! It is unnatural! It is A SIN!' Luckily, I had to swoon to the ground at his feet then, and his huge stomach hid the fact that I was laughing uncontrollably. By the end of the rehearsal, we were all limp as rags and cursing West right and left.

One of the people who is being coached by him is a boy called Joseph O'Connor, who is just eighteen, lives in Putney, is a Catholic and has no money. We get on fine and during lunch hour we sit side by side on the steps and talk about the Old Vic, which he adores, about Olivier and John Gielgud. We have quite the same opinion about John's legs, slinky walk, flaring nostrils and his strange noises, etc., and we both agree that Larry's legs look gorgeous in riding breeches. He asked if I knew the Embankment cafés and we compared notes about the Blue Cockatoo and the Lombard. Sometimes, we go out together and have a cheap lunch in Soho – spaghetti and Coca-Cola.

Thursday Four days to the RADA test but I'm not too nervous. Old West seems to be quite happy with me. Last night I heard the *Count of Monte Cristo* on the wireless. The piteousness of youth in a snare, dropped into a nightmare pit of loneliness in the dungeons of Château d'If. I listened to the sound of his sobbing in the echoing darkness, chill and dank, so still that he hears the blood throbbing in his ears. It is these things that lay their hands tight and sudden on my heart. I could never marry a man older than me.

Monday Today I did the RADA test with old Barnes, who runs the place, watching from his box. Felt as sick as a cat, but still had to go on and say my opening line, 'Oh, I feel marvellous now!' My gosh, what irony. But to my intense joy, they only heard the first piece and just as I was preparing to do Viola, Barnes called out, 'You needn't do any more, my dear, that's quite enough.' As I was going out, I heard him mutter to his friend, 'That gel could be quite pretty if she took her glasses off.' Apparently, according to one of my friends, that means I have definitely got in.

Spent the next day in glorious relaxation, dressing gown, cold cream and curlers like a dirty old char. Mummy came back that evening from Anglesey where she was staying with her friend Isla, the one who has to shave twice a day. She is relieved to be back as she fears that Isla has developed a lesbian passion for her.

Tuesday West has just rung up. I HAVE GOT IN!! To celebrate, I raced down to the King's Road and had my hair set for five shillings at a cheap little shop by a Scotsman who was wearing lots of rings and insisted on breathing heavily down my neck. After that, went to see the Marx Brothers for the first time in *Duck Soup*. They are complete geniuses, especially the dumb Harpo.

I got back to find Sid writing her Apologia in the drawing room. Her fringe is gradually being pushed up into a wild red halo. She says she is going to carve me a pregnant Madonna in limewood, with the corn growing up and curving back towards the centre of gravity, her womb.

It was mid-November, and I was already beginning to think about Christmas. I was hoping there would be no interference from those boring old charities. Alas, my hopes were soon dashed. Dermot, Sid's father, had written a nativity play titled *Chorus Angelorum*. He had hired a West End theatre and over Christmas was planning to give several performances for charity. There were professional actors involved, but the shepherds and angels were to be played by me and my friends. Naturally I was keen to play the role of an angel but, no, I was to be a boring old shepherd in a ragged brown tunic. Thetis and Hilary, of course, were angels.

The other night a few of the people involved in the play came round and had dinner with us. One was a dark young man around thirty, his face disfigured by a harelip. He is called Greville Knyvett and is going to be the conductor. I found him incredibly interesting, the most lovely and unusual character – very simple and crude with no poses. I might even find him attractive – in spite of his harelip – if he wasn't so old. After dinner we had a concert. Mummy and Sid played their ukuleles, Henry played the piano and I sat on my little musical chair rocking to and fro and making strange tinkling noises. Greville conducted and I noticed he had beautiful hands.

When it was over, he squatted on the floor like a schoolboy, beckoned me down to him and showed me a trick with pennies. We lit our cigarettes from each other's stumps and flicked them into the wastebasket and discussed Freud. My God, he's interesting. I don't remember too much of the conversation, I was too busy drinking sherry and smoking to keep my nerves calm and my hands occupied. I was also busy getting adjusted to him . . . It may sound heartless but I make a point of showing a different self to everyone I meet according to what they are like. Not that the sides I show are unreal poses. They're just different moods and facets of one thing. It is most useful. One should be 'all things to all men'. I have no fixed character. I am a chameleon. I can appreciate and become part of almost anything if I want to.

Soon I was feeling as familiar with him as if I'd known him all my life.

He has a way of very lightly laying a hand on my shoulder as he speaks and he treats me like a grown-up. Just before he left, he invited me to go round to his flat next Tuesday for dinner – alone – to hear his Ravel records. Well, of course, Mummy's hackles rose. The idea of my going alone at night to a young man's house without a chaperone! Sid tried to explain to her that these arty people always invited you round at night to hear music and talk and there was nothing naughty about it, but Mummy was firm.

Nevertheless, I noticed that Greville said goodbye to me in a much more intimate way than he did to the others.

Monday Still *furious* with Mummy – if it hadn't been for her I would have spent the whole evening alone with him. Why is it that the one person you're supposed to love the most is always the one who upsets you most? Oh, God! If only I was grown-up and could go out with friends where and when I liked. Sometimes I wish I could leave home and have my own little room in the same house as friends who have an absorbing and common interest in acting and music. That is the kind of life I'd adore.

Tuesday Three days in bed with a stinking cold! The first rehearsal for the shepherds is next week so I've got to get well soon. In the meantime I console myself with the occasional cigarette, eating liqueur chocolates and reading Ouida. Her books are the funniest things I have ever read! Oh, boy! Her descriptions of high life! Such as Bertie Errol, the darling of the thirties, always breakfasting off lobster cutlets à la Maréchale or curling a loose leaf around his manila. They are all such terrible men with terrible moustaches! '"What? Not seen la Vavasour? Mon cher, you have yet to live," yawned Arthur de Bennus, Viscomte and Chamberlain du Roi, wiping his long perfumed moustache as he rose from the Baccarat table and drank down some iced chambertin.'

Thursday Mummy's birthday. Grand reception in darkened room and presents laid out by candlelight. Played Mummy in to 'Silver Threads Amongst the Gold' on the piano – not a very popular choice! Henry's present didn't go down too well either – machine music by Mossolov called 'Steel Foundry', which Henry says is the latest thing. Mummy was horrified and said she could do just as well banging on her toothglass but I thought it was lovely.

Monday First rehearsal for the shepherds. Greville conducting in his shirtsleeves and a dark pullover, a lock of hair falling over his forehead. The electric lamp dramatised the hollows of his very subtle and attractive face. Conducting with his hands poised, slim flexible wrists and a signet ring gleaming on his little finger, he sways on the balls of his feet. Then comes a quick strong downward swoop of the stick – 'Forte, for-*te*. Now!'

When I am not on stage, I crouch in the orchestra pit, watching his every movement. Sometimes, he will

come and sit beside me and we have the most
wonderful conversations. He has given me back a love
of music, which was poisoned for me at school by Shar.
I *want* to listen to symphonies and classical music and
educate myself for *him*. I play the piano every day now
and sing Schubert's love songs.

Hilary, shedding her angel's wings, has come home
with me to stay for a few days. She hasn't much news
except that Father Stapleton, her Irish parish priest, has
tried to seduce her several times (unsuccessfully).
Tonight, we went to a very dreary cocktail party given
by Thetis. A lot of boring French boys talking about
Jean-Paul Sartre. Mummy got very drunk on four dry
Martinis and we drove home singing and hooting
lewdly. She said everything felt like a Wembley
switchback!

Christmas Eve Snow for four days, thick and unceasing,
pipes all frozen and nothing to do. Midnight mass.
Henry had indigestion. Presents from family: *Plato's
Republic*. A cameo brooch. A live grass snake!

New Year's Eve Henry, Sid, Mummy and I went to see
the New Year in. We fought our way through a
seething mob to Eros. Everyone with paper hats
and balloons, dancing in circles, singing, climbing

lamp-posts, cheeking the mounted police and jeering at the unfortunate limousines that were trying to struggle through. Everywhere, searchlights and flashes of newspaper men taking photos.

Eros seemed almost God-like, poised in a glitter of brass on one foot, half in darkness, half in light, with the velvet beams of the searchlight on him; beneath his immortal gaze, all London made whoopee. Everyone singing 'Auld Lang Syne', dancing in a ring. When midnight struck, there was such a roar that the bells and cannons were drowned. And overhead, with tragic irony, the news repeated over and over again in moving lights, 'War in Spain still continuing. Serious fighting.' But nobody was watching.

New Year's Day I am in love with Greville Knyvett. I am in love with his eyes, his face, his hair, in love with his posture and his height, his hands, his mannerisms, even his strange voice. I am in love with his rugged simplicity, his deep emotional fire that he keeps in check – in love with a certain austereness in him, in love with his laugh and the way he swears. In love with the nearness of him and his touch, in love with his smile, his mind, his being, his soul, his lovely and intensely interesting character. I am hungry to sound him to the bottom – to know more of him – but as soon as our play is finished, he is going on a three-

month tour of Scandinavia. I have given him my
address but I don't suppose he'll bother to write
to me.

The last day of the play We all said sad goodbyes. I thought
he might give me a proper kiss but he only gave me a
farewell peck. Now all I have to look forward to is
going to RADA.

Sunday Today I cried all the way through Mass,
thinking about Greville. If it wasn't for Mummy,
I could have gone to his rooms, seen his books,
listened to his music and got to know him. Now
he's away for three months and I may never see
him again.

My first day at RADA was memorable with the whole
place buzzing like a beehive. Before I was allowed in,
there was lots of paperwork for me to do so I had plenty
of time to examine my fellow students. They seemed to
divide roughly into three kinds: arty, tarty or smarty. The
arty boys had long hair, the arty girls long skirts. The
tarty ones were wearing lots of makeup and the few smar-
ties tended to stand in separate groups, looking down their
noses at us.

I was delighted to see my old friend Anne Dawson
again as I'd heard she'd joined a repertory company in
Kent. Apparently she'd only been given two parts, a can-
can dancer and a deaf woman in a trance, so she'd been
only too happy to come back to RADA, where she
thought her talents would be more appreciated.

I'm glad to say that after only a week, I'm already
beginning to feel at home here. The Academy is huge,
with two theatres, lots of rehearsal rooms and a café
selling awful food, where we seem to be spending a lot
of time criticising and tearing to shreds the acting
abilities of our class mates. I think I'm going to enjoy
myself here – it's just like being back at school all over
again – all the friendships, the playing the fool and
having fun, without the unpleasant work. I am getting
to know the streets around the Academy. We all have
our special favourite shops. Everyone meets at the
snack bar in Store Street, has their hair done at Jo-Jo's
(very cheap), goes to the bookshop over the road, buys
stockings and lipstick and peanuts at the Goodge
Street Woolworths.

Our two favourite restaurants are Domenico's, if
you're flush, and Economo's, very cheap and dirty.
Anne and I go every day to the second-hand bookshop
next to it. We look at immoral books on the barrow

outside and roar and scream with laughter quite
without shame. Anatole France's *Reine Pedarque* is a
present favourite. All the illustrations show the heroine
either getting out of or into bed with a young man. It
must be a singularly monotonous plot.

I'm in something called Class A with a very
interesting set of people. According to RADA
tradition, we've given them all names. Alan Sykes is the
Gorgeous Creature. Will Squire because of his hollow
cheeks and slanting eyes is the Faun. There is also a
painfully thin girl whom we call Night Starvation. My
old friend Joseph O'Connor is with us. He never says
goodbye, but yells 'Away and mock the time with fairest
show!' so for obvious reasons he is simply known as the
Ham. As for Bill Bennett, he is so safe and reliable he
doesn't even merit a name!

I can't decide which of the men I like the best.
Joseph is like a beautifully iced cake, thrilling to look
at but deadly dull once you get into him, although I
rather like the way he wiggles his ears up and down
when he's nervous, like a rabbit. Alan Sykes is such a
wonderful actor that his looks don't matter. I thought
at first that he was just a nice ordinary boy, but he is a
revelation on stage. A different and thrilling personality.
I love to sit and watch his face and movements and
hear the husky caressing undertones of his voice. On

the other hand, I find Will Squire, little Faun, incredibly attractive. I have been noticing him more and more, with his high cheekbones, big slanting eyes and his rough sea-green shirts. I think now that he is the most attractive man in the Academy, more exciting than Joseph or Alan, very young, vital, impish and intriguing. Sadly, I haven't managed to speak to him yet.

The plays we are doing for the term are *As You Like It*, *Macbeth* and *Romeo and Juliet*, and I have got Rosalind in Act II where she first arrives in the Forest of Arden.

We are also doing *School for Scandal*, which will be fun. Ballet classes are lovely, terribly hard, but I get a thrill from watching the better pupils doing it.

Today we met our producer, a fascinating man called Ronnie Carr. Just to hear him talking about the characters or saying the lines is as good as a review. He also has a trick of playing the piano whilst talking to us, kind of 'Chopsticks' accompaniment to his sarcastic and rather brutal criticism, his main *bête noire* being the unfortunate Joseph. Today, watching Alan going a bit over the top, I heard Carr mutter to one of his neighbours, 'Mr Sykes is suffering from a bad attack of O'Connoritis.'

Later, in *Romeo and Juliet*, Faun's death of Mercutio evoked frantic applause. But Carr obviously thought he was overdoing the moans and writhing around on the floor. He said, in that slow inexorable way of his with a gleam in his eye, 'It seems to me, Mr Squire, that the pains you are suffering from could quite easily be remedied by a large dash of – er – Eno's!'

He seems to have taken quite a shine to me and, at one point, called out, 'Come and talk to me about your inhibitions, darling!'

During rehearsal, his favourite position is to sit with his legs splayed out over five rows of seats, cigarette dangling from his mouth and his back to the no smoking sign whilst rasping out orders like 'Make your entrance with more panache, Duke,' and 'Don't stick your behind out, Miss Bruce-Day.'

In the afternoon, we had mime with Miss Pisk – black pants, Russian jacket, very sweet and foreign. We each had to come out in turn and give a rendering of a pregnant girl in church, praying for forgiveness and finally staggering into the aisle to collapse from remorse and/or morning sickness. The men had to do a man going mad in a cell. Alan, with much twitching of the mouth and beating on the walls; Bill, a cynical gleam in his eye, giving a pretty good imitation of the lion house at feeding time.

One thing had been making me unhappy. Although I was seeing him every day, I still hadn't had a chance

173

to speak to the Faun. But then a lovely thing
happened: I was waiting to go home at the fourteen
bus stop and he came up with a few friends but didn't
see me. I ran up to the top and he came in last. I
looked at him and he looked back. Then his face
broke into a smile and he said, 'Haven't I seen your
face somewhere before?' I thought, I should think so,
seeing I've been tracking around after you for days.
Anyway, he left his friends and came and sat beside
me, leaning over the back of the seat in front of me,
and talked and talked. When he got up, he said, 'See
you tomorrow,' and left me sitting there in staring
ecstasy.

Wednesday Fencing today in the Little Theatre. I knew
Faun would be there so bagged a seat right in the front.
To my delight, as soon as it was over, he jumped the
footlights and sank into the seat next to mine, pulling
off his fencing shoes which had holes where his toes
came through. As he leant down, I could feel his breath
on my forehead. I longed to cool my face against the
hollow of his cheek. We talked and Faun showed me
the real workings of his mind for the first time. I
realised, almost to my surprise, that he is extremely
intelligent. He discussed how Shakespeare builds up
his scenes like a piece of music with introduction and

motif, climax and coda. The rest of the day passed like
a dream. Luckily it was mainly unimportant stuff, such
as elocution.

Monday Mime. Miss Mackintosh, who drinks like a fish
and has vocal cords sodden with gin, arrived quarter of
an hour late, completely drunk, her toque crooked, her
veil on one side, over a pallid face with red-rimmed
eyes. We were frozen with horror, but had to go
through with it. I stood badly and Mackintosh said,
'Deportment ish the mosht important thing on the
shtage!' and staggered reeling into a chair. No one
dared laugh but really it was very funny. Luckily, the
subject today was 'Falls'.

Tonight, a nice Ballet Club boy drove me home in
his little Austin. 'There's room for your arse and a
bottle of Bass and the rest of you has to be forced in,'
he sang. Then he speeded round the park to show off
and nearly finished the car off altogether.

Tuesday William Devlin took our rehearsal this morning
and infused some of his own dynamic energy into
us . . . It's a funny thing, but I've yet to know an actor
or producer who didn't lean up against the no smoking
sign with a cigarette in his mouth. A sort of tradition,
I suppose.

That night, listening to the radio, I chanced upon a performance of the Comédie Française of *Cyrano de Bergerac*. It lasted till midnight. I got undressed and sat up wrapped in a bedspread beside the wireless. Never having read or heard it before, the impact on the emotions was quite terrific. I lay on my tummy with my eyes tight shut and cried with excitement.

Wednesday Auditions for this term's *Macbeth* with Miss Carrington. She is piquant, dry, dramatic, rather fascinating. Joseph got Macbeth. I got Lady Macbeth, one of my favourite parts in Shakespeare. I thought I'd knock their eyes out, so I looked Joseph straight in the face and said with the utmost relish, 'I have given suck, etc.' and I got the part.

The next day I fought my way into the gallery during a rehearsal of the second year's *St Joan* and he was sitting on the balustrade with his hands thrown out against the wall. In the faint glow from the stage, his cheeks seemed even hollower, his eyes brighter. I gradually worked nearer to him till I was sitting on the ledge next to him and every time my hand or shoulder touched his it was as if an electric shock ran through me.

His face is the queerest, weirdest and most unusual I have ever seen, like something magical out of elf-land and I shall never tire of it.

Friday Rehearsing with Carrington is great. She takes us alone and we think out new moves, new inflections and nuances. She works you up to a pitch of almost hysterical excitement, gripping you round the body, pinning your arms to your sides and hissing out her instructions in a tense monotone. You stiffen with emotion, and the words boil out of you like red hot metal. Later we rehearsed with Joseph, who was in fine form, barnstorming his whiskers off. In the murder scene, he made strange noises as if he was about to be sick, reminiscent of Gielgud in his salad days.

The Weekend Thank goodness we had a proper roast lunch this weekend. Mummy seems to have got bored with starving for charity. As soon as I get home, I always look to see if there's a letter from Greville. I've written to him twice but so far he hasn't answered. I suppose I must now admit he has forgotten me altogether. All the same, I believe in miracles, I can never quite give up hope. I don't know who I prefer, Greville or Faun. They are so utterly different – Greville is far away from me in the past, and the present is here between my two hands. Now that I am in love with Faun it makes it easier for me to come to grips with the fact that I shall probably never see Greville again.

After dinner we listened to W. H. Auden's 'Ascent of F6' on the wireless. It was very interesting although I didn't understand a word of it.

Monday A crowd of photographers arrived from *Picture Post* laden with lights and cameras. In the canteen, everyone was sitting around trying to look vacant, beautifully got up, and pretending not to know that the photographers were around. Alan Sykes was leaning over the table, his eyes dreamy, delicately sniffing at a large blue iris, Anne was displaying her legs and I was pretending to be studying Shakespeare.

It's a funny thing but Faun has a queer and lovely smell about him – like no other person. I think it's his cigarettes which he's always smoking. But there's something else, vaguely scented, which I can't trace. I know he doesn't put anything on his hair, which is thick, brown and wavy, so it's not grease. Well, this smell is like a fox's scent to me. I can smell it a mile off. I never even need to wear my glasses because I can always tell where he is even with my eyes shut. The other day, I was in the cloakroom, thinking about him with the door shut, and suddenly I smelt Faun. I was out of the door like greased lightning and, sure enough, there he was. As we passed each other he stopped and gave me a singular look. I wonder if he knows? On the stairs behind him, I could see some papers scattered on the floor and I knew immediately that they were his. Without hesitation, I seized and pocketed them.

By the light of the lamp near the bus stop I read them. One was a letter from his mother, a stumbling, unpunctuated and illiterate letter, which almost made me cry. They must be a poor common family, Will, their pride, their white hope – an amazingly pathetic letter. I'm going to put a ten shilling note into the pocket of his coat if I can manage it.

Tuesday Today I spotted him, having coffee alone in the canteen. As the letter was in my pocket still, I went up and asked him if it was his. He seemed very pleased and asked me to sit down with him. Slowly and cautiously, I began to draw him out and soon he was talking about his background without any self-consciousness. His parents live in Swansea among the coalmines in the distressed areas and they have no money. Faun has kept himself since he was sixteen, working on the roads, breaking stones, and doing any odd jobs he could get.

He used to dread the summer when it was so hot and the work was so hard. Later he worked in a bell factory where they made everything by hand, from church bells to the kind you get on ice-cream barrows that play three notes.

179

He had acted in a lot of amateur plays, so then he got the idea into his head that he could go up to London and be an actor. His friends and parents thought that he was mad but he went all the same and got a LCC scholarship with two pounds, ten shillings a week to live on. Of course at first he had a terrible inferiority complex, thinking he would be an absolute outsider and everybody would look down on him. After all, he had no breeding or money, no education, no background. So when he found how nice everybody was, he was terribly surprised.

Of course he's different. That's what's so special about him. The first thing I thought when I met him was that he was unlike any other men I had ever met. It was as if he had dropped untouched from another sphere. A boy who has never danced, never seen a camera before, never played games or learnt to speak French or any other public school achievement. He is fresh, young and very vital, nothing stale and nothing cynical, with a natural intelligence and an alert mind. He has the tang of a Cox's Orange Pippin and I love him very much.

When I got home I was sneezing a lot so Mummy put me to bed. I think I must have caught Faun's cold. It's rather nice to think I may have one of his germs inside me.

I adore *As You Like It*, and as for Rosalind, if I never
played any other character, I wouldn't care if I could
play her. I don't have to change myself to be her, she is
inside me. Me and Ellen did our scene alone with
Miss Carrington. We got worked up, I did it fine,
loved it and Miss C was frightfully pleased, said I
was first-rate, that I had the personality and looks for
Rosalind and that we both realised the fun and light-
heartedness of the scene. Oh, how I enjoy doing it.
How I understand it.

Monday We have a new girl in our class, Marietta, a
Viennese. Very gloomy and neurotic. 'My God,' she
keeps saying, 'how unhaarrrrppy I am! All we Viennese
are unharrrrppy.' We discuss Life with a capital L while
eating crab sandwiches and crumpets. Of course it's all
a pose and we are much more interested in the
crumpets really than the Meaning of Life.

At last, a Modern Play! It's called *Dinner at Eight*
and is not very interesting but it's got a real kitten
in it, which I can play with whilst waiting to go on
stage!

Tuesday Faun's hair is getting longer and longer and
longer. I guess he needs the price of a haircut. I slipped
half a crown into his pocket the other day – it's the

only way I can relieve my feelings. When he's excited, his hair hangs down either side of his face like the soft brown ears on a little dog. I'm fascinated with Faun's hair. I feel wild, not being able to touch it.

Sunday Got a bit bored so went to the Ballet Club alone. During the long intervals, I went into the ladies' and read *Crime and Punishment* on the lavatory seat. It is a wonderful novel, sordid and great. I think Raskalnikoff has a character rather like mine.

Saw *Dark Elegies* – a new, strange and unbelievably moving ballet, quite different from anything I'd ever seen, in fact it might have been a new school of dancing altogether – everything stark, new, strange, and unbelievably moving and beautiful. It concerned young peasant men and women mourning for their dead children. Every movement had a symbolism: it was, in fact, perfect 'significant form'. It was as much a revolution in choreography as *L'Après-midi d'un Faun*, or Stravinsky's *Rite of Spring*. Frank Staff was outstanding both in technique and interpretation. I'm afraid I may be getting a crack on him, which gives me three at the moment, Faun, Greville and Frank.

What a silly word 'crack' is. I would like to say 'in love with' but it is not considered either right or possible by the romantic British public to be in love with more than two people at the same time. I, on the contrary, could love sixty at once if I chose. I can't understand this attitude for no two men are the same, and you love each one for something different. Of course, it depends a lot on which one you're seeing most of at the time. Is that heartless? No, it is having too much heart. Too great an amount of love to give. I ought to have been a courtesan in a Watteau/Fragonard setting, beautiful – of course. (Of course!) And with plenty of choice. Then I would have the chance of letting off all my surplus libido.

Wednesday Anne and I had lunch at a snack bar – spaghetti and Coca-Cola – and talked about sex. Discussing whether she would go away for the weekend with a man if asked. I said yes, I thought it would be fine, provided he was nice-looking enough. She told me she is in love with Joseph! Why is it that it is always the women who are in love with the men and never the other way round? I didn't want to talk about Faun, so I told her about a strange and rather worrying experience I'd had the other day. While we were rehearsing *As You Like It* Alan, who has been very friendly to me for the last few days, came up to me in the wings, put his arms around me while murmuring poetry in my ear with his face only an inch away.

At the feel of his body against mine, the strong masculine warmth of it, beads of sweat coming through the greasepaint, and the very touch of the hairs on his arm against my skin, I felt quite faint with pleasure and I know it would be the same, I told her, with any man who had any physical attraction for me. I know lots of my friends who say men have no physical attraction for them at all. So I suppose I must be peculiar. Anne says not to worry, it's the result of our being repressed by the convent.

In the evening we went to Shakespeare's Birthday Festival at the Old Vic. When the curtain went up there was John Gielgud standing against a plain backdrop with his legs apart looking up into the flies with an immobile gaze which never wavered once during the prolonged applause that greeted this dramatic manifestation. Then, slowly lowering his eyes, he broke into a *Hamlet* soliloquy without further ado – 'but break my heart or I must hold my tongue'. As he neared the climax of the speech, tears glistened in his eyes and rolled down his cheeks. Good old John! He always knows how to make an effect. The audience simply ate him up.

Esme Percy's Othello was simply frightful, spitting all over the stage and all over the poor boy who played Iago. But what sticks most in my mind is

Ernest Milton's Shylock, in *The Merchant of Venice* —
not old and whining but a straight tall eagle of a man
eaten away by inward fires, with the most amazing
eyes burning like coals in his pale face. He spoke very
quietly but just once or twice his eyes snapped into
blazing fury. The audience was noisy and extremely
enthusiastic.

Thursday Today we had a ballet class. The dust rose in
clouds in the gym. Every window was shut and the
heat was insufferable. There was a sort of rasping
gritty noise as twenty pairs of pink ballet shoes
scraped on the sandy floor, tottering in arabesque.

During afternoon rehearsal Jean, who plays the lead
in *Dinner at Eight*, suddenly introduced a new bit of
business into her bedroom scene. While putting her
stockings on, she pulled her négligé up higher and
higher, hunting for the suspender, which completely
paralysed O'Connor and made him dry up three
times. Carr leant over the balcony and called down, 'I
think you'd better cut the stockings bit altogether, my
dear. Mr O'Connor appears to be in a swooning
condition.'

It was around this time we had our first glimpse of
the Greek play *Electra*. We were hoping it was going to
be as funny as last year's *Trojan Women*, which by all

accounts was a riot with a few bricks being dropped offstage to represent the fall of Troy and the crash of burning towers. We were not to be disappointed. The first rehearsal was a dream. The stage was full of weird females with their hair in bags (the Chorus), striking poses and uttering strange incantations, and embarrassed young men in short tunics with knobbly bare legs. The old girl who taught us was deaf, with hollow eyes and long white hair. She staggered round the stage under an imaginary amphora, gazing out front, and murmuring, 'Orrnward! Orrrnward!'

Then the first Electra emerged in horn-rimmed glasses, shorts, check coat and boots and commenced, 'Dark shepherdess of many a golden star!' in a strong American accent. Joseph did the first Pylades, an awful young man who doesn't have a word to say throughout, but has to look appealing and intelligent nevertheless. He draped one leg round the other and put one hand on his hip. If Orestes expressed an opinion, he nodded gravely. If Orestes mentioned the setting sun, he shaded his eyes, struck an attitude and studied it with intense interest. This reduced us to fits of uncontrollable laughter.

Monday Marietta has never explored the streets around the Academy so Jean, Anne and I took her to

Woolworths and bought some sweets and some braces
to keep our tights up – then we ate Welsh rarebit in
Store Street. Jean had only got sevenpence to last her
for the rest of the week, so we had to feed her in turn
off our forks. I lent her enough to get home with, and
then we wandered around, very happy, looking at shops
and saying which dresses we thought would suit us,
and Marietta told us about how she had her first kiss
the other night when a boy took her to see *Hamlet*, but
apparently it hadn't been so hot. (The kiss, that is, not
the play.)

I hear O'Connor is, in fact, twenty-five. No wonder
his ideas are so mature.

Tuesday In the evening a performance of *Dinner at Eight*.
The dressing room was sheer bedlam with clothes
strewn everywhere, the kitten being sick on a piece of
newspaper, the sardines for its lunch decorating one
corner, its earthbox in the other. Faun, who was
rehearsing next door, rushed into our dressing room in
his red Mercutio wig, hanging on to his tights, and
asked if anyone had any halfpennies. I sprung up like a
tiger and had given him four before anyone had time to
move. He twisted them into the top of his tights,
thanking me. I wished I could have made them
shillings.

Wednesday Dress rehearsal for *As You Like It* in the evening. Wild excitement – wore a lovely short green velvet tunic with a golden chain and hanging sleeves. I was lousy in the travelling scene but very good in the scene with Celia. I got so excited in my scenes with Orlando that I nearly choked. We all enjoyed it and did well. Joseph looked handsome but fluffed his lines. Alan played beautifully but looked a bit sea-sick in pale makeup. Lots of people came up afterwards and congratulated me. It's true. My Rosalind *is* good. Because, of course, I understand her so well, being in love myself. I do the whole scene where she first hears Orlando is in the forest with an ecstatic inner love burning inside me and it comes out in my voice. I can only act well in parts that call for deep intense feelings. I have too much of it in me anyway. Parts that require comedy technique leave me cold. It's a pity. I must try and cultivate comedy, it is very necessary.

Mummy came to see me perform and was frightfully impressed. She had been expecting something awful but had a pleasant surprise. I'm usually in a ghastly state of pessimism about my work but now I feel more confident.

Friday Anne and I went to see *Dark Victory*. Bette Davis is the greatest actress on the screen now or ever.

Tuesday Rehearsals with Carr. As for Faun, not for the first time I felt a most extraordinary bond stretching between him and me. A kind of silent intercourse that had no need for words. Sometimes it goes, and that is because we are frightened of each other. The other day, watching his death scene as Mercutio in *Romeo and Juliet*, I had to cram lozenges into my mouth to give my teeth something to grip on.

Another strange thing is that my appearance has been changing without my noticing it. I suppose it is an unconscious adjustment to his personality and tastes. Not that he's ever voiced them. Nowadays, I don't wear lipstick, rouge or nail polish any more or curl my hair much, and I can't stick anything except the plainest oldest dresses and I don't wear stockings or good shoes. In fact I should look awful, but funnily enough, I like myself rather better this way.

Home tomorrow! End of term depression has set in. In the afternoon we all went to Domenico's café to try and spin out the last minutes of term a little bit longer. We ate fried egg sandwiches while discussing the different merits and faults of our fifty-odd classmates – a highly stimulating activity. When the acting reputations of our friends lay around the table in rags, we turned to the men and talked about who was in love with who. About midnight, we said goodbyes and our goodbyes were many and lachrymose. Jean came with me to the bus stop and we embraced there being by this time thoroughly emotional and drunk.

Saturday To the Zoo, which I hate. Can't bear to see caged animals.

Sunday Went to Caledonian market. Lovely antiques.

Monday Dinner at Thetis's. Her mother, who has now dyed her hair auburn, was throwing around epigrams and practically fainting because I said I loved Chopin. After supper, Thetis and I went to the new Zola film *La Bête Humaine* – sex, train smoke, strangulation and suicide, but mainly sex, all the way – the burning devouring sensuality of the French!

Wednesday Decided to go to the Ballet Club. Standing in the foyer, I heard a funny nasal voice some distance away. Greville came to my mind and I began to visualise his face and wonder when I would see him again. Then the miracle commenced. I turned and there he was. It was him. He was walking back to his seat in the front row with a woman. It was like hell as I knew I wouldn't have the courage to speak to him. I didn't think that he would have remembered me. Then at the

bar during the second interval, Greville's friend, dear
Peter Pope, waved to me with his funny little smile.
Hello. How's Joan? I answered stumblingly – silly little
platitudes. Then he flicked his eyes a little to the side
and I knew a kind of landslide had begun and would
end in my undreamt-of dream. There was Greville,
smiling at me. I took his hand, not knowing what to
do, and I pretended to have forgotten his name. Peter
murmured, 'Greville Knyvett,' and by the sound of his
voice and the look in his eye, I knew that *he* knew that
I knew perfectly well what his name was. I could have
kissed Peter as he discreetly vanished, a good fairy
with glasses on the end of his nose and a twinkle in
his eye.

We were left alone, and he took up the thread of
our acquaintance as if it was only yesterday. I thrilled
as he put his hand on my shoulder. I felt as if I was in
a dream and had to put my hand on the radiator to
make sure I wasn't.

At last the ballet came to an end and we were
together in the foyer. He said, 'Wait for me while I get
my hat.' Peter, passing, raised his eyebrows in
unfeigned delight as if to say 'What ho!' and vanished
into the night. Greville returned wearing a broad-
brimmed black hat and looking divine. He was
swinging a quite unnecessary black umbrella in a wild

way that made it dangerous to walk near him. He pulled me into a shop doorway out of the wind to light my cigarette and our faces were close together. Then we were joined by the woman he came with. I felt exceedingly hostile towards her. We measured each other's lengths like two hens strutting around a solitary cockerel and I observed with pleasure she had a face like a pudding. Then he took down my telephone number and we made plans to go to the Wells one night. I felt here my dream reached its culminating peak of bliss. He was actually going to take me to the ballet! The possibilities that had just opened up were endless.

My bus came and as I clung on to the rail, looking back, he swept off his hat and made a low absurd bow. I was bursting to tell someone but had no one to tell, so I sat in my nightdress in front of the mirror and talked to myself far into the night.

Wednesday Greville has rung and asked me to go to the Wells with him tomorrow night. And could I manage to get away in time for dinner before it? I said I would if I had to throw a fainting fit. 'Meet you outside the Chinese restaurant at six thirty!'

I don't think I'm in love with him any more, but I'm very fond of him indeed. It's a pity, but one always loves what one hasn't got. Once you get it you cease to want it in the same way. That's how it works. Once you've got the man, penetrated the mists and mystery, where is the joy and the thrill? 'Where are the snows of yesteryear?' Well, perhaps I shall fall in love with him all over again when I see more of him. At the moment I feel I'm happy in his company and excited. I feel love but I'm not in love. At least, I don't think so.

More than anything else, I feel triumph. Triumph over the evil fates of my life. The triumph of the cat who's stolen the cream, the collector who, having given up hope, has his rare specimen handed to him on a platter. Now my ego is re-inflated. My inferiority complex has received a setback. Instead of looking like death, as is usual first thing in the morning, I descended radiant and starry-eyed in more senses than one as I had curled my lashes and was wearing smart clothes again. I think I *could* be in love with Greville properly if I saw more of him. It might be rather fun – though life with two raging loves would be a bit hectic. All day at the Academy, prowling after Faun. All evening waiting for Greville to ring. His nasal voice gives me a morbid pleasure. I was very much younger when I first fell in love with him. I feel at least six years older now than I was last year.

Whether this will affect my feelings for him or not, time will tell.

Two weeks later Because Greville is so much older and more experienced than me, I keep hoping that he might kiss me but he never does. In fact I'm beginning to find this relationship a bit disappointing. Dinner, drinks, the theatre and that's it. I suppose he still thinks of me as an innocent little girl.

Friday Dinner with Mum. Afterwards went round to Greville's room – he was alone and we played *Dido and Aeneas* on the gramophone while G conducted, I thought beautifully, with a baton. He has a trick of lulling you with gentle motion then letting the stick leap out with unexpected grace and vigour.

His bookcase is a glorious mixture. *The Adventures of Sherlock Holmes*, the poems of D. H. Lawrence and *A Practical Guide to Astral Projection*. About midnight, we ate cherry cake and peppermints and made tea with some milk that had turned into cheese in the carton. Next Friday we are going to see *Tristan* at Covent Garden.

Friday Thomas Beecham greeted with roars and hoots
of applause. In the interval we went to Lyons and had
sausage and chips. Greville made the mistake of telling
me he had just bought first editions of James Joyce's
Ulysses and *Finnegans Wake* for five guineas apiece. After
that, I let him pay for everything without a single qualm.

Sunday Sid and I visited Granny's grave at Eastbourne.
Sid in her worst mood and I was feeling a bit rough
too. The result was we made jokes in the worse
possible taste all the way there in the train and became
hysterical with laughter when we couldn't find the
grave. For quite half an hour we played a kind of
ghastly hide and seek, amongst flapping crows and
incredible angels, wandering along asphalt pathways in
a high sea wind – in fact a mild form of T. S. Eliotean
hell. Sid behaved very badly at the graveside and we
had a hard job keeping on our faces of gloom in front
of the sexton.

Tonight Greville and I had dinner at the Cowboy,
double deckers of lettuce, mayonnaise, olives and
cheese which absolutely finished me, then we staggered
into the gallery queue for *Of Mice and Men* where I met
Anne D. My God, the Apollo is the lousiest gallery in
London. Absolutely no room for your bottom at all.
Anne, who had had an injection in her behind that

morning, went through agonies. It sure was worth it though. It was one of the best plays with the best acting I've seen for a long time. Tomorrow it's back to the Academy so Greville and I said our goodbyes, but still no kiss! I'm wondering if I'll still find myself in love with Faun on my return or will I find him just a commonplace high-spirited young animal? Well, I'll be finding out tomorrow!

First day back at the Academy No sign of Faun. Then while I was waiting for ballet class in the upstairs corridor, I heard running footsteps and Faun came hurtling around the far corner and raced down the corridor towards me. As he came nearer, there was a sudden flash of recognition and a welcoming smile. Nothing was said but as he vanished down the stairs, I felt my heart thudding with excitement and I knew then that nothing had changed.

We spent most of the week rehearsing. As usual, student rehearsals in the big theatre were a total farce. Whenever there was a sentimental scene, people would yap like dogs, give wolf whistles or, worst of all, suddenly black out all the lights on the stage. Group rehearsals were quieter but could be very chaotic, with students knitting jumpers, sitting on top of the piano, surrounded by dirty teacups, making rude remarks about the actors and me cutting the pages of my new sixpenny copy of *Fleurs du Mal* with a nail file.

Saturday To the Old Vic for Guthrie's full-length modern dress *Hamlet*. Alec Guinness played Hamlet and a lovely job he made of it. He was terribly thin and wasted-away-looking, a queer face, a lovely smile and ears like a young bat. He was very young and unaffected. No ranting and roaring, but moving, quiet realism – with touches of delicate humour and at times an unbearable pathos, as of something lost and bewildered. He had the quality of being able to stand still and yet arrest the attention – slow unhurried moves, and then stillness, nothing fussy or unnecessary. When he had quietly finished his first soliloquy, he drew out a silk handkerchief from his sleeve and instead of wiping away a tear, calmly and deliberately blew his nose. This so enchanted me, that I wanted to stand up and clap there and then.

Monday A marvellous surprise awaited me. In dancing class we are going to be doing a pavane and today Miss Fletcher was putting us into partners for the whole term. 'Now, who's left over – Miss Wyndham? Well, Miss Wyndham, you'd better dance with Mr Squire . . .'

I broke out in a cold sweat and saw Faun holding out his hand to me. He pretended to kiss mine, acting, as we do all the time, then we danced down the entire length of the gym.

Later, he asked me to rehearse the dance with him, so I took his hand and we started. The joy in my heart was so steady and full, pressed down and flowing over, pressing like a tide against my ribs, I don't know how I kept my voice steady. He has no sense for the rhythm of steps at all. Holding his hand I taught him like a small child, like a hen teaching her chickens. 'One two three, *four* five six!' When we were tired, he sat down and confided he'd never been to a dance in his life. Couldn't if he was asked. He just hadn't got the feeling for rhythm in him. We are practising every Monday from ten to eleven and I am bringing in some music. This is the best thing that has happened to me since I came to the Academy. I can't rant and become hysterical about it like last term. It's something deep and peaceful in the core of my being. He was most apologetic about taking up my time when he was so bad. If only he knew!

That night a divine cynical Jewess gave us a talk on what makes us laugh at dirty stories. We decided that it was expected of us – a sort of social gesture.

Tuesday I have made an amazing discovery. Miss Carrington is a lezzie! Showing Lily how to do a sad farewell kiss, she suddenly crushed her in her arms, and pressed her lips on Lily's with terrible force. I felt quite sick for a minute. Not because Carrington is disgusting, she is very attractive, but because it seemed so unright. At the same time, I must admit, it fascinated me. The rest of the day we rehearsed *Dinner at Eight* and I was forced to watch Faun doing a love scene with Sheila. When she touched his hair, I tore at the flesh on the back of my hands and left marks like cat scratches. As a result, I did my Millicent scene with so much anguish and abandon that Carr made me play half of it with a book on my head like those girls training to be debs.

But the rehearsal I enjoyed the most was *Electra*, with me and my friends in the chorus and Faun as the messenger. He rushed on, one arm held above his head, as smooth as marble with a vein running up from the wrist, not at all like Bill's hairy ones.

However, drama quickly gave way to farce, as it usually does in these Greek plays. In the last scene Bill and Alan had been picked as the bier carriers. As usual, they grabbed the first willing body to hand, in this case, Ed, the carpenter. They didn't realise how heavy he was and the bier got dropped with a most tremendous thud. An audible cry of 'Christ!' rang through the auditorium as the shroud slipped sideways, a pair of bony feet revealed at one end, Ed's grizzled face at the other. At this point, the unfortunate Electra had to lean over the body, murmuring, 'Ah, that girl-like face.' The gallery was in hysterics.

My admiration for Faun has blazed up amazingly during these last few days. It's much worse than ever before and I can hardly bear to be out of his sight. I don't give a damn for Greville any more. I've come to the bottom of him, and I've come sooner than I expected to. I think he was a sort of trial flight. I mistook a candle for the sun and leapt up crying, 'It's day!' He's shallow, and I wouldn't care if I never saw him again. He is utterly inferior in every way to Faun. I love Faun in a kind of universal way, I love him as God loves the world, as a mother loves her child. In fact I've never felt so ruddy maternal in all my life. I can remember saying I could be in love with ten men all at the same time. Heaven knows what I meant by *that*!

Monday Went at ten for a dance rehearsal with Faun. I waited for him in the sitting room in a howling draught. The door had been left open, so I would see him coming up the stairs. I waited and waited, then in

despair I wrote the following execrable verses if you
can call them that.

> You are my friend and you
>   do not know me.
> You are my life, and you do
>   not love me.
> As the Sun knows not the
>   grain that it ripens,
> The husk that it breaks
>   Even so, unknowing, you
> Ripen the grains of my heart.
>   Could you not leave them at rest in the earth
> Not burn them, break them,
>   Bringing forth
> This flower of loneliness
>   That aches in the sunlight?

Well, then he came, which happily cut short this flow
which could easily have gone on indefinitely, becoming
more and more mixed as regards its metaphors.

Two weeks later Faun, Joseph, Anne, Molly and I have
formed a group of friends called the Gang. Every day we
have terrific discussions during the lunch hour. Yesterday
we fought over whether it was right to give money to

201

animals' homes when there are men starving. We three were for, Molly and Faun against. Faun has the power of words. He argues like a man pleading in a matter of life or death. Intensely keen and forceful, hands gesticulating, head close to yours. When exasperated, he bangs his head on the table and groans with despair. Joseph argues in a deep philosophical strain with occasional flashes of whimsy, illogical humour delivered with a disarming child-like logic. He was very convincing on the subject of whether animals have souls. Molly, who was against it, was more and more worked up, almost hysterical, pulled his hair and flung pepper in his face.

Today we discussed modern civilisation. Joseph is extremely cynical about it and says we are decaying fast and have no great artists left. He hates all music after Beethoven and thinks the only thing left worth anything is the miracle of science. He says the language and the people's minds are dead too. I stood up for modern music, but had to admit that, as a civilisation, we are pretty lousy. Joseph was born a few centuries too late. He would have made a perfect Elizabethan.

Saturday Anne and I are giving ourselves a rare treat today. A matinée of John Gielgud's latest *Hamlet*. The first time we saw it we were both at school and both fell madly in love with him.

The Lyceum is a gorgeous and unique theatre, huge, cavernous, gilded and tasselled with the atmosphere of one's first pantomime. John's Hamlet has matured beyond all recognition. He has simplified and pruned it of all unnecessary tricks. It is now down to bare essentials and moving beyond all words. His voice is unnervingly beautiful. To quote James Agate: '"This brave o'erhanging vault, fretted with golden fire" hung in the air like a jewel.'

In the last act, when he foresees his death, that last 'let be' sent Anne and me into a state of utter ecstasy, hugging each other as the trumpets blared and the curtains swung back for the final fight.

He died standing, the most wonderful death scene that's ever been seen, or so we thought. He seemed to keep himself up by willpower alone, a swaying figure taut as a steel wire, stretched to breaking point. 'The rest is silence' was almost soundless. For a second, he stood almost completely alone, bloodless, confronting eternity, then fell back dead over Horatio's arms. Afterwards, he made a short and very tired speech to the audience. A very emotional evening.

Monday Today, rather to our surprise, Faun brought some of his early poems for us to look at. He told us they were a parody of the ultra-modern poets, with little pieces of his own soul chucked in. In fact, bits of

it were pure T. S. Eliot, plus lashings of Edith Sitwell
and Ezra Pound. They really were perfect examples of
the 'dead cats/cesspools/grave worms/gasometer' type
of verse. He describes human nature as a

> Nerve-rotten deadness
> Stinking like fly-blown fish.
> Rot-high and sour
> Grey wastes of *hoi-polloi*
> Flooding the scene
> Background, cathedral
> Foreground, latrine.

This burning searing bitterness is almost incredible in
so young a man, a mind in rebellion against humanity
and civilisation. Life must have been treating him very
badly just then. How much of this is serious and how
much just sheer beautiful caricature was difficult to
decide. When the true mind of Faun breaks through, it
is of extraordinary clarity and beauty, as in his poem,
'On a Graveyard':

> Chill air drops to chillier stones
> Where florally minister the black-clad groups.
> The flesh dies, as does the soul
> In this walled citadel afloat the heath.

I was rather impressed by this. Quite honestly, I didn't
know he had it in him. I couldn't have written anything
so clever. To think I used to liken Faun to a fool, just a
lovely fool, no intellect!

During lunch, we talked about love. Joseph doesn't
agree with love whilst at the Academy. He said you
can't think of anything else and your work suffers.
Faun disagreed. He said being in love 'makes you more
aware of life, you feel more deeply and you suffer more
and you act better'. Is he in love, and if he suffers, is it
unrequited? I do hope so.

Monday Rather surprisingly, Marietta has joined our
group. She has stopped being so miserable ever since a
dago propositioned her at a cocktail party, though she
still says stupid things like 'I didn't know women were
allowed to wear trousers.' On the whole, though, she is
fitting in well, and starting to enjoy herself at last.

Tuesday Today the whole of our division is in a state
of hysteria: the term's biggest excitement has finally
arrived, our various parts for the dreaded Mid-Course
Test having been put up. Everyone raging, complaining,
jealous or triumphant, muttering in corners. Whoever
did the choosing must be bats. For instance, Pam Tiffin,
the best actress in our class, has been given Miss Arden,

whose most dramatic moment is to announce, 'There
are six in the waiting room, Doctor.' I had been hoping
to get Juliet but that little bitch June Atkinson has got
her. Serve her right if she gets Bill Bennett as Romeo
but at least I am doing a bit of Lady Macbeth with
a lovely dress to go with it. Faun, luckily, has got his
death scene as Mercutio, and a little bit of Orlando
thrown in. Of course, we are not on speaking terms
with those who have got our parts in the other classes,
but go around being witty and sarcastic about them
at every opportunity. It's a hell of an atmosphere.

Tuesday Dancing. We practised the interchange of
looks. Old Fletcher yelling, 'Smile! Smile at your man!
All pas de deux should be conversations.' I didn't find
that particularly difficult with Faun.

Then at two, Joseph, Anne and I went to the
Theatrical Garden Party. It was hot and breathless and
our clothes stuck to us, but Ranelagh was cool and
green. We wandered round for a bit, but all the time I
was looking out for Faun. Suddenly I saw him. He was
wearing the same grey sackcloth jacket that smells of
the roads. It'll drop off him soon.

We all stayed together for the rest of the afternoon,
wandering happily, the green grass swimming before us
endlessly. Then I went on the roundabouts but Faun

wouldn't – he said it would make him ill. The heat
from the engines, the heat of the sun, the loud
grinding music and the whirling rhythm of the horses,
Faun's face, laughing, thrown up at me each time I
swung past, gave me a feeling of intense happiness,
almost faintness. I clung hard onto the reins and was
glad when the music stopped and Faun was holding
out his hand for me to jump down.

After that we went in those little Dodgem cars that
you bump people with and I chased Faun like a demon,
landing some good hefty bumps on his mudguard. We
were quite hysterical by the end of it and my stockings
were in shreds. Then Joseph spotted Noël Coward in a
grey topper with a carnation in his buttonhole. He was
auctioning ladies' underclothes and had just succeeded
in selling a most immodest pair of panties which he'd
autographed for Godfrey Winn who looked the most
awful poomp. But Coward was just superb. Talk about
magnetism. The way he was going on about those
pants made us almost die laughing. After that we ate
ice-cream and drank cold lemonade out of bottles.
Then, to my indescribable joy, the other two said they
felt tired, and left. We saw them to the gate and turned
back alone together.

First we lay on our tummies in the cool shade
behind Doug Byng's tent and had a smoke, listening to

someone inside jazzing on a piano, then we wriggled up onto a bank in the sun where the grass grew long. We stretched ourselves out and Faun laid his head on my arm. I watched the grass throwing long thin shadows across his brown face. I realised that if only he turned his head a quarter of an inch to the right, his lips would be against my skin – but sadly he never moved, so instead I plaited a daisy chain and put it on his head. He looked like some ridiculous wood creature, garlanded with flowers and drunk with the sun.

We felt no need to talk. I know no other man with whom I so enjoy silence – with others I feel uncomfortable and try to make conversation. With Faun, everything is all right. We talk when we want to, otherwise we keep silent.

Finally, after weeks of frenzied rehearsal, the day of the Mid-Course Test arrived. There were hours of boredom in a hot dressing room that resembled the world in the process of creation, wildly crammed and untidy, with everyone fighting for the mirrors, borrowing greasepaint, losing things, singing, laughing or wailing with apprehension. Clouds of gold dust floating over everything; a yapping Pekinese under the table, people sewing white heather into their pants for luck; people sneezing and having to turn round three times to avert misfortune. Smells and heat and noise and superstitions and headaches, with beads of sweat coming through our greasepaint and cold tea spilt all over my dress.

In the cool vaults under the creaking stage, prop baskets loomed dimly. On the stage itself, groups of people were being intense to an empty theatre, while three judges, one of them drunk, sat above them in a lighted box. Carr has been very kind and helpful, giving us little pep talks about our worst faults and how best to avoid them. He warned me again about wobbling my head and told me to spend half an hour a day walking around with a book on top of it. He told Faun that he ought to use his own personality more on stage and not be so shy. 'No, you're not one of those men with round beautiful faces and nothing behind them. You've got an interesting head and an interesting personality. Get rid of your inferiority complex!' Faun threw back his thin, neat, square shoulders and listened, his head bent a little to one side like a sparrow. Anne, who had to cry on stage, was told to eat nothing all day, then think about her mother dying.

When the time came for my Lady Macbeth, I got into my peacock blue dress with a full skirt, long red plaits, a purple veil and a golden crown. I gave myself a

deathly pallor with lots of green eyeshadow, so I
looked evil and decadent, like a green and gold asp.

I was horribly nervous but soon found myself
coming to life in a brief but impassioned glittering
existence. No one was more surprised than myself.
Joseph was good too, lurking around in a long black
wig and moustache with a purple cloak and awful
leggings.

Faun came next in his fight scene as Mercutio.
I watched, tense with excitement, and when the
dagger went into his side, I felt a physical shock,
almost pain, as if the blade had actually gone into
me. I'd never felt this before. As the life went out of
him, I had the feeling of something terribly hurt and
taken unawares. His acting has improved enormously.
When we did our little scene from *As You Like It*, his
Orlando was something totally new. Instead of the
usual rather heavy romantic lead, there was something
quite puckish about him. He rolled on the ground
and shook with silent laughter at Rosamund's
playacting, let her rumple his hair. You felt that
if there had been a tree on stage, he would have
climbed it. I found this singularly refreshing
after more ponderous Orlandos.

What followed next was total farce and came as
rather a relief. Molly was doing Hamlet's mother in the

closet scene and wore a huge hoop draped in purple
silk. When she rose and turned to make her dramatic
exit, the audience gasped with horror to see a large gap
all the way down the back, with drawers and
suspenders well in evidence. After the first shock, we
roared and screamed with laughter especially when
poor Hamlet said, 'Thus bad begins and worse remains
behind!'

After the show, Anne and I sat down for a nice long
gossip. Soon we began to feel hungry, having had
nothing all day except a cheese stick, a raw carrot and
two chocolate creams that tasted like railway soap. We
were busily discussing what restaurant to go to when,
to our horror, we discovered we'd been locked into the
big theatre.

We climbed onto the fire escape, took off our
shoes, slung our makeup boxes round our necks and
scaled an eight-foot trellis into the College Hall
garden. I got cramp and Molly complained of pains
around her heart. I thought she was going to pass out
there and then among the begonias, leaving me to
spend the night on the lawn with a stiffening corpse.
Luckily she recovered and climbed the trellis on the
other side where she stood on the top rung in full
stage makeup, her skirts blowing up round her head
and yelled for help. Miss Finch, the hostel manageress,

heard her and put her head out the window. Finally she descended in puce velvet and pearls and let us in, covered in grass, earth and greasepaint.

Home for the weekend Mummy is behaving rather strangely at the moment – she seems worried all the time and is listening to the wireless a lot. Something about Germany, I think. I couldn't be much help to her, as nobody in the Academy has been talking about politics recently. We're only interested in one thing – whether our performances are good or bad. To escape the atmosphere of anxiety, I went to the cinema with Molly, who talked non-stop about her sex life in a loud voice all through the organ interlude. Fortunately, the Marx Brothers' *Night at the Opera* came along to shut her up. One of the funniest films I've ever seen.

Tuesday Only two more days to the end of term!

Faun and I have now reached a wonderfully calm and relaxed stage in our relationship. We are now the best of friends and his mind is often strangely in touch with mine.

Last night, I suddenly felt an urge to read Marlowe again and sat up half the night over *Dr Faustus*. Today at lunch, he said, 'I love Marlowe. I was reading him all yesterday and last night. *Tamburlaine* is just noise but

Faustus is fantastic.' When I told him I had been reading Marlowe too, a kind of ray passed between us, a feeling of wordless, binding intimacy.

Thursday Last performance of *Electra*. Faun was only a member of the chorus but there was a great moment when with his arms raised, his eyes wide and gleaming, he cried, 'Throw me a Thessalian blade, this Dorian is too light.' My heart went up like a rocket. He lifted the whole play, pulled it together and silenced the gallery.

Carr tells me I've got excellent marks for Lady Macb and everyone is very pleased with the progress I've made this term. We said goodbye to Carr. Faun made an emotional speech and we gave him a fifteen shilling book token. He told us he was very sorry to lose us, as we had been the nicest class he'd ever had. Then I spotted the notice: 'The judges have awarded the Mid-Course Test prize of five pounds to William Squire.' I immediately grabbed hold of Bill Bennett, who had charge of the tote, and caught him bag in hand, on the point of welshing with the sponduliks. I duly extracted one and fourpence from him, my tote winnings on Faun getting the prize. Everybody seems delighted that he's won. In fact, he seems to have become a cult figure. Anne thinks he will go far, 'though of course his looks are against him'. I gazed at her in stupefied amazement.

The most beautiful face I've ever seen and she thinks he's ugly? She probably thinks a ghastly film star like Clark Gable is good-looking.

In the afternoon, there was a last performance of *Dinner at Eight*. I played Hattie in a full-skirted velvet dress and silvered my hair at the temples. For the last time, I swept about the stage, manipulating a cheese straw and a cigarette, drinking cold tea and pretending it was whisky. After that we rested to be ready for a special performance of *School for Scandal* for teachers and staff only. By half past seven, we were all up and packed into the dressing room making ourselves look glamorous with our silver wigs, white makeup with black beauty spots and, of course, lots of fans.

Apart from the theatre, the house was now empty and deserted. Everyone had gone home. And yet I could smell Faun! Outside the dressing room, I picked up the scent and I thought, He has passed this way only a few seconds ago. I ran down the stairs, holding up my skirts, raced through the passages, pushed open the door leading to the gallery and came face to face with him. The only student in the whole Academy who had stayed for our show. He looked up from the cigarette he was lighting and gave me a welcoming smile. I sat down next to him, wondering if I was in a dream, but we were soon talking, leaning over the gallery bar, our heads close together.

Then the play started, and when it came to my first entrance I was so keyed up, knowing he was there, that I just swept on and gave the only good performance of Lady Teazle that I'd ever given. I got laughs where I'd never got them before – I delivered my last lines with a venomous hiss: 'May your husband live these *fifty* years.'

I sailed out, flung off my wig and ran straight upstairs. I knew that my hair was hanging dank with greasepaint but I didn't care. I ran straight up to Faun. 'Was I all right?' I asked. Out of a mist of words, I heard two things that turned the world to gold for me. 'I'm so glad I stayed to the end. It was worthwhile just to see you. You were wonderful. The way you spat out those last words!' And he meant it, he was quite quiet and sincere. Then he asked me if I was in the next act. I honestly think he would have stayed if I had been. As I wasn't, he thought he'd better go. We lingered a little at the door, talking about how it was the last day. Then he said, 'Well, goodbye, Joan. See you after the holidays.' My hand was hanging down near his. Suddenly, so my heart nearly stopped beating, he took it and held it, gave it a little squeeze, then was gone.

He knows I'm in love with him. He must do! I sank
down into his seat, which was still warm and suddenly
dropped my head on my hands in a burst of
bewildered ecstasy and cried and cried with happiness.
My face was burning and sticky with greasepaint under
my fingers. I felt I would choke and ran out into the
passage and back to the dressing room. We all kissed
each other, said goodbye and scattered for the holidays.
I thought, This has been the happiest day of my life –
a perfect ending. I expected nothing and got so much.

I boarded the bus as if it was a golden chariot and was
still in such a state of excitement when I got home, my
mother probably thought I was quite mad. I'm sure she
must have wished she was my age still and capable of such
ecstasy.

16 July 1938 Summer hols at last. I was looking
forward to them so much but in fact I'm feeling a bit
bored. I miss all the gossip and the excitement. Even
the daily discipline. With no work to do, I've had to
fall back on ballet, theatre and cinema. To make matters
worse, there's a horrible atmosphere of unresolved
tension in the air – everyone worrying about the
possibility of war with Germany. Am missing Faun
terribly.

Only one new thing – despite all the worrying, Mummy and Sid seem obsessed with Russia and go to Russian Masses. Today they took me to one and it was beautiful. We received communion in both kinds, holding up a red cloth under our chins and sipping warm wine out of a golden spoon. Afterwards we were given a piece of bread to clean out our mouths. The only snag is you have to stand for two hours.

Henry has introduced them to a superb Russian priest who comes to tea a lot. Almost too good to be true – he might have stepped out of a Cecil B. de Mille film. He has a long black flowing beard, a wonderful pale face and an aquiline nose, and wears a long black robe with huge hanging sleeves with a heavy silver crucifix round his neck. Even when devouring quantities of liver-sausage sandwiches, he still manages to look like Rasputin. Of course, being obsessed with all things Russian, we went to see Chekhov's *Three Sisters*. It was wonderful and so depressing we nearly committed suicide ourselves from the power of suggestion! The best thing in the play was the pathetic young Baron, Michael Redgrave. So shy and awkward, with his clumsy abrupt movements, nervous, high-pitched laugh and blind, tender adoration for the beauty of Irina. It seems to be only inevitable that so helpless and dear a creature should be crushed. He

217

seemed the very essence of all the nice young men we know, all a little helpless and incapable of dealing with the world. I cried myself to a pulp during the awful last scene, and emerged looking like death.

My Academy report has finally arrived. Horrors. Barnes says I have a 'certain frail charm'. Frail – me? That's really too much coming from old Barnes. I felt quite embarrassed showing it to Mummy and Sid.

The Russian theme continues. The Ballets Russes is visiting, so I went to see Baronova in *Les Sylphides*. Each time I see this ballet it seems infused with more beauty. She seemed to be evoking all the spirits of the air to draw her over the stage without touching it. When the houselights went up and she and her partner Dolin came out in front of the curtain, one almost expected them to fade and crumble into dust, so much had they become a part of the moonlight.

Beau Danube with Massine was a dream. There is a moment when he stands utterly still in the middle of the stage, just before the waltz, and slowly raises his head. Sitting in the gods, looking straight down on him, I felt I was drowning in those great eyes, like pools of green water.

After the show, although it was dark and raining, we queued at the stage door for autographs. The dancers were very friendly and seemed glad to see us. But still no Massine.

Then, just as we were giving up hope, there was a sudden hoarse yell and he came out with a Russian bodyguard. He was wearing a brown coat and soft hat and looked very young and entirely sweet. I was right in front of the queue by this time, pressed up against him, almost in his arms. I got my book signed and felt his breath on my cheeks. In the queue behind me a bunch of Communists were singing rude songs about the horrors of what they call the 'Karist Regeem'. There were also some beautiful arties who positively made your stomach wince – or your heart. One young man had long wavy hair almost down to his waist!

Saturday Met Aunt Olivia for lunch. She charged out of four restaurants because they didn't have licences and we finally ended up in a commercial hotel smelling like a morgue where she drank large Scotch and sodas. She told me lots of dirty stories and we got the giggles so much we were quite glad to stagger out into the daylight.

Monday Only one thing is worrying me. Although I loved the Russian Masses, so romantic and picturesque, I still have my old doubts about religion in general and the existence of an all-good, all-powerful God. I still imagine God and the Devil, squaring up to each other, one black, one white, but both equally powerful. I'm a Manicheeist, I suppose. Anyway, I've been avoiding confession lately and last week I lied about it, and Sid caught me out. Now she's worried about the state of my soul, and yesterday I was dragged off, reluctantly, to a religious seminar on the meaning of good and evil. The church hall was crowded with young, serious-looking students, all listening attentively. I felt like someone in a cocaine dream, moving among tiny people.

On the stage were two Dominicans, discussing the nature of sin. Father Strauss affected an air of bored inattention, behind which he listened with all his brain. Father Gilbey, with cherubic smile and acid tongue, rolled out scholastic terms and Latin tags luscious on the tongue. Most of it went straight over my head but even when I didn't understand it, the 'purring of invisible antennae' stimulated and amused me. But I still remained unconvinced.

8 *August* A quick trip to the cottage where Mummy has had a small extension built on. It is going to be a proper dining room and put an end to that boring old 'tray life' as we used to call it. There is also a new lavatory next door to the bathroom. Sid disapproves strongly. She thinks they are far too near together and

says, in her usual coarse fashion, that she doesn't want
to be lying in a nice hot bath listening to Henry
making noises like a horse next door.

After the cottage, we visited Isla, my mother's great
friend, in Wales. They grew up together and, judging by
photos, spent most of their time in fancy dress. Red Indian
seemed to be a favourite, with Mummy a dashing
Hiawatha to Isla's Minnie Ha-Ha. The result was Isla's passionate devotion to Iris, which lasted the rest of her life.
Although my mother was very fond of her, she found this
passion extremely embarrassing, so our visits were cut to a
minimum. I was sorry about this, for I found the whole
place quite heavenly. Isla's house was high up over the
Menai Straits with trees to the water's edge and the sailing
boats on the blue sea as white as if they were cut out of
paper.

Isla herself I find a bit of a bore, but luckily, she's
feeling bilious and stays in bed most of the time. All
her henchmen, on the other hand, are absolute angels,
very simple, earthy and humorous. Mackay, the butler,
is so sweet, I could eat him! So is Harold, who sails the
boat. He is like a brown monkey and smells exactly like
Faun. I suppose it's the smell of work ingrained in
their clothes and skin.

I have become the complete 'hearty' down here,
striding out in the dew before breakfast in corduroy
trousers with a stick, a whistle and two dogs, and then
down to the farm to feed the cows and see the newborn
calf. Then back for a breakfast of kidneys, bacon and
pickled herring, followed by a few rounds of clock golf,
finally taking the rowing-boat out for a cruise around
the outlying islands, with binoculars slung round my
neck, and no makeup. Horrible metamorphosis!

On a more genteel note, we also sold produce at the
Vicar's bazaar, raffled teasets at the Conservative fête
and made conversation over tomato sandwiches at
various county tea parties. I've also been climbing the
mountains around Snowdon. So bleak that nothing
grows on them but the sparsest grass, with thin streams
running down into the hidden lakes, and sheep lying
curled in the rock crevices. One of the lakes is supposed
to be bottomless but I fell into it, so I can positively
state that it isn't; it's shadowed by red-berried mountain
ash. Mountains almost reconcile one to Wordsworth.

Today we took the boat out fishing but didn't catch
much. Shoals of rose-coloured jellyfish undulated past
us in the clear green water. A porpoise showed its back
three times, snorting loudly. Later we went to Puffin
Island – quite bare except for a ruined monastery. The
lighthouse nearby booms out a single note on its bell

every minute. I went for a walk among the bracken and met a tame white she-goat who ate my chocolates. Coralie, Isla's horse, won its first race today, ridden by little Dukie. Later we had a bit of a party where he and Mackay exchanged endless toasts.

Sunday Home by the midnight mail. I felt dreadfully sorry saying goodbye to Mackay. He is the nicest butler who ever lived. Imagine an English butler coming upon you, half naked, in a hammock, capering round you, and swinging you into the air with chuckles of glee. 'Go to sleep my *ba*-by'. He drove us to Holyhead to catch the mail. With the air of a naughty schoolboy, he opened the throttle and let her do eighty miles an hour.

Later I stood on the docks looking down at the oily water. A little before midnight, we saw two lights, one above the other, moving quite far out. They were on the mast of a ship coming back from Ireland. She had turned off her engine and was drifting in slowly and silently with the tide. Her sharp prow cut the glittering water, the light glistened on her wet rails and on either side of the prow were long slanting eyes like those of some gentle sea animal. As she came nearer, we could see her name in white – Cambria. A man on deck threw a rope with a single strong unfurling movement.

No one spoke a word. She moved into the dock, within a few feet of the landing stage, with a kind of silent dignity and stopped dead at her appointed place. There had been no sounds throughout, and I had never seen anything so lovely. Then, within five minutes, she disgorged a crowd of exhausted-looking women with their babies and a hungry-looking Irish priest who talked to us about coursing. Then we were taken to our sleepers by Jim, a nice Scotsman.

The rest of my hols are to be spent at Orchard Close with Grandpa Guy and Auntie Violet – Violet more voluptuous than ever with a green bow in her auburn-dyed hair. Grandpa Guy, whom I call Poppa, is still in his same favourite chair doing his crosswords and listening to Wagner. But both the boys have changed beyond recognition. Hughie has stopped going round like a gangster, with a plastic toy gun, and has developed a passion for the piano. He was delighted to find I could read music, and we play duets together. Francis is beginning to grow whiskers and looks faintly phosphorescent around the chin, like some plant growing under a board away from the sun. I can hardly recognise him as the boy I used to play with.

In the evenings, there are often charades or we dance to the gramophone. Our favourite tunes are 'Blue

Moon', 'Red Sails in the Sunset' and 'Dancing Cheek
to Cheek'. I love dancing, but prefer to dance alone.
My hands mould and shape the music in the air and
draw it to me. My limbs are no longer under my
control. They go wherever the music takes them –
effortlessly and ecstatically.

Ingrid, my little half-sister, is here, being looked
after by Violet. Dick had only wanted a son and heir
to inherit Clouds so he callously farmed her out to
her grandparents soon after she was born. Inkie, as
they call her, is very piquant-looking, rather like a
Monet painting. Her thin gold hair is worn straight
and reaches her shoulders. Her eyes are brown and a
lovely shape. She has two pet mice she adores. She
leans her face across the table and she and the mice
wuffle at each other, the mice's noses quivering, Inkie's
little nose wrinkled in wonder and affection. After
watching them for a bit, I felt inspired to write a
poem – as follows:

To stroke with sensitive hands a young and silken
    mouse.
To feel the warm sleek life flowing under the fingertips,
Throbbing through the slim body, sheathed in ashen
    fur.

★

How comfortable a mouse!
Compact and curled into a drowsing curve
Of passive bliss.
The pink feet fraily furled,
The shell-like ears close-set
And quiet whiskers tremulous no more.

How delicate a mouse!
Delicate in running, delicate in yawning
Bright needle teeth
Globed eyes of liquid jet
And tendril tail round-curling at the tip
Most satisfying MOUSE!

Last night I went up to Inkie's room. She sleeps
with her old nurse, whose possessions consist entirely
of numerous holy books and a phial of Phul Nana
perfume. She told me that when she grows up she
wants to be a ballet dancer or an actress.

Big surprise! Dick on a flying visit. He roared up the
drive in his black and red racing car and took us off
for a spin in the countryside at eighty miles an hour,
with the wind like a wall in our faces.

He also promised Inkie that as a special treat he
would take her to see the film *Snow White and the Seven
Dwarfs*. Unfortunately he got bored halfway through

and walked out. What a selfish monster my father is!
Such men should not be allowed to live.

The holidays are nearly over and I'm longing to see
Faun again. Last night I had a beautiful dream about
him. It is amazing the depth and sweetness of feeling
you get in dreams. It was almost perfect. I dreamt I was
lying beside him on a cold spring morning, my hand in
his, but when I woke I found I was alone.

1 September Back to London. After the peace of
Orchard Close, it seems like a different country. The
air is electric with what I call 'war-worry'.

At Violet's we hardly ever read newspapers or
listened to the wireless. Occasionally, we would talk
about Hitler and the possibility of war, but only in
terms of jocular disbelief whereas here they talk of
nothing else. October 1st is known as 'Der Tag', the
dreaded day when Hitler's ultimatum will run out and
he will invade Czechoslovakia. If we were to oppose
him, there would be war.

We went to the cinema to see *All Quiet on the Western
Front*, on with *Ten Men and a Girl*. The house was packed.
Everyone in a worked-up condition because of recent
events. This anti-war propaganda found a ready
response. The boy next to me was sobbing with his
head in his hands and everyone cheered and clapped

when the characters denounced the futility of war. I
realised that it was the most colossal madness ever set
in motion by mankind. The film spared you nothing.
Hand-to-hand fighting with bayonets, bodies on the
wire, men mowed down by machine guns, bomb upon
bomb. Horror, gross brutality, filth and mud. No
spark of glory or chivalry, just stark terror, butchery
and purposeless destruction. How sane human beings
can do such things to each other, I don't know. One
could only ask, in vain amazement, 'Why? In God's
name, why? What's it all for?'

Can any violation of treaties or loss of prestige
justify it? Surely not. It is too horribly unnatural,
bestial and pagan.

You see a company of eighteen-year-old boys being
sent mad and killed one by one. Finally the last
survivor crawls out to touch a butterfly that has
alighted on the broken earth by the dug-out and is
shot by a sniper. The most pathetic scene in the whole
film.

Over the weekend, I made the mistake of
mentioning RADA and saw my mother look at me
with shocked disbelief. 'RADA?' she said. 'You don't
honestly think I'm going to let you go back to RADA
while this crisis lasts, do you?' Apparently if there was
a war, I'd be evacuated immediately to the country and

in the meantime, she's keeping me firmly under her wing. I was totally devastated but managed not to show it. That night I cried myself to sleep, although I simply cannot believe that I won't be going back.

On the first day of term, I was allowed to go back just to collect my makeup box and I was in the hall when I saw Faun and his friends come tumbling down the staircase. He waved and called out to me, but I pretended not to see him. They seemed so happy to be reunited, a little male nucleus with no need of women. I am madly envious of them and wish to God that I was a man so that I could reach Faun on his own ground, as a friend, go out with my arm around his shoulders and no one to care. None of this damn sex making me frightened and ashamed to seem too affectionate. What a lousy thing it is to be a woman – oh, God, I wish, *I wish* I was a man. Then I could be Faun's friend – and experience that real unembarrassed friendship of men, unpassionate and yet intense with no coqueterie, no barriers. Oh, well, what's the point of dreaming?

I stepped quietly through a side door and realised I would perhaps never see him again. This is an unbearable thought – but I still hope that if this crisis passes, which it surely *must*, now that Chamberlain is going to see Hitler, everything will become normal again and I'll be back at RADA.

Sunday, 18 September Went to Hyde Park to listen to
the tub-thumpers. There was an Irishman with a
nutcracker face, waving a Free State flag, a socialist
with a face like a charming weasel, spouting left-wing
politics with a quiet yet biting sense of humour.
There was every nationality, from Negroes to
Spaniards, and fanatical women who screeched,
'Listen, my dear one!' and preached emancipation.
The *Daily Mirror* has two posters: one with WAR in
black six-inch letters, the other PEACE with seven-inch
ones. These they interchange every so often. Luckily
it is peace at the moment while Chamberlain talks
with Hitler.

26 September Der Tag is now only three days off. We got
our gas masks this morning. It was horrible to see old
women struggling to pull them on over their buns.
Mine is lovely. It makes rude noises like a horse behind
my ears. We also puttied up the gasproof room today.
Mummy can't eat. I eat twice as much. My old
schoolfriend Thetis sends a very superior letter saying
how stupid it is for us to take this thing seriously and
how she hates the English. Sid says she'd like to give
her a good kick up the bum. Sid's so vulgar sometimes
but I do agree with her. What a bloody life. Here I sit
with a gas mask glaring like a death's head from the

mantelpiece, and Aunt Olivia having hysterics in the room below.

Wednesday 28th Everyone still plunged in doom and gloom. We heard Hitler giving a roaring, ranting speech on the wireless. Wonderfully staged. Old Goering brought him on like a tenor, cannons booming and the band playing Wagner. Then dead silence and Goering's *'Der Führer sprecht!'* He nearly broke a blood vessel over Beneš, the Czech prime minister, and became tearful with a broken voice over his beloved Sudetens. The crowd was like a wild beast chanting 'Sieg Heil' and 'Hang him' (Beneš). After he had finished they sang 'Deutschland Über Alles' and gave way to mass hysteria.

September 29th Darling Chamberlain has gone to see Hitler again with Musso and Daladier. Pray God it's successful. He told us we mustn't worry. It will be all right this time. He is the sweetest man and looks just like a kind llama. Mummy couldn't sleep all night: the aeroplanes and guns were so bad she thought the war had started. Early next morning, she woke Sid just before it was time to go to church and asked her to get a paper.

Sid came up the stairs as if she had seen a ghost. I came out in my dressing gown and saw the *Daily Mirror*

headline from the top of the stairs. 'IT IS PEACE!' Sid
told me, 'Don't shout,' and went up to Mummy, who
started crying with relief.

After the strain of the last few days, the minute the
tension relaxed, we felt so tired we could hardly walk.
But we went to a Mass of thanksgiving at Westminster
Cathedral. The lighting and décor were horribly
theatrical and the marble pillars looked like something
from the temple scene in *Aida*. When the old Cardinal
swept in, his red train carried by little boys, he
reminded me of Wolsey in Henry VIII. It's awful the
way I think of everything in terms of the theatre!

It was Sid's birthday so after Mass when we'd read
the newspapers with all the good news about the
success of the conference, we had a riotous birthday
breakfast with pâté de foie, candles and gramophone
records, and piles of presents and flowers to celebrate.

30 September Went down to Buck House to welcome
good old Neville home. Dense crowds and pouring
rain. A lovely sunset and a purple searchlight on the
Palace. We mobbed the car and yelled and screamed,
'Good old Chamberlain! We want Chamberlain!' until
the King and Queen came out with him onto the
balcony. Then we gave them all we'd got and sang 'For
He's a Jolly Good Fellow' and 'God Save The King'

while he waved and smiled and Mrs Chamberlain wept with emotion. We were in real Armistice mood. I found myself hugging a complete stranger, a very charming and good-looking man who drove us home in his car.

On the way back we passed Piccadilly Circus and saw more crowds celebrating, dancing and singing, '*No war! No war!*' and 'Doing the Lambeth Walk, *oi!*'

Later that evening, Henry rushed in, red with excitement, seized my hand and said, 'Peace be unto you,' and proceeded to parody Italian opera in a riotous fashion for the rest of the evening. I laughed so much I got a pain. After dinner, I went up to my room, fell on my knees and said my prayers. The first in a long time. Thanking God in his mercy for granting us 'peace in our time'.

Then I lay in bed, thinking about my future.

Maybe I'll be a famous actress with my name in lights.

Perhaps I'll be married to Faun with lots of lovely Welsh children.

On the other hand, I could just be something boring, like a nurse or a typist. But whatever the future may bring, my best hope will be to wake every morning, happy and thankful to be still alive.